Spring Com

By Jorian Jenks

Spring Comes Again

By Jorian Jenks

Copyright © 2012 Black House Publishing Ltd

All rights reserved. No part of this book may be reproduced in any form by any electronic or mechanical means including photocopying, recording, or information storage and retrieval without permission in writing from the publisher.

ISBN-13: 978-1-908476-85-2

Black House Publishing Ltd
Kemp House
152 City Road
London
UNITED KINGDOM
EC1V 2NX

www.blackhousepublishing.co.uk
Email: info@blackhousepublishing.co.uk

PROLOGUE

THE WINTER OF OUR DISCONTENT

WHEN we feel most in need of guidance, let us remember the Divine manifestation of Nature. For Nature is one of the very few real and permanent things in this world of ours.

Empires, civilizations and philosophies rise and fall, but nothing deflects by a hair's breadth the ever-recurring cycle of life. The young corn spears bravely on our English uplands just as it did thousands of years ago in the valley of the Euphrates, as it will do thousands of years hence. The beasts of the field bring forth their young in due season, to beget and bear in their turn. Generation succeeds generation, as life gives place to death, and death to new life again.

So turns the wheel of human endeavour. Neither to man nor his works is granted the immortality of godhead; he is born not to achieve finality, but to struggle unceasingly towards it, destined ever to travel hopefully, never to have arrived. As the Cross is his sure sign of redemption and final reward, so the eternal miracle of the seasons is his sure sign of life and hope ever renewed.

When he is most oppressed by doubts and fears, when the future seems most pregnant with ominous uncertainties, he must remember that winter never fails to give place to spring. We cannot name the day when the first buds break, but break they will. We cannot fix the date when the earth first moves with renewed fecundity, but we know that it will not fail to bring forth its increase. If we have but the faith to look forward, we need not mourn the loss of the past or bemoan the sterility of the present. For spring will come again.

We are witnessing today the closing stages of an era. The political faith which inspired and upheld our fathers, and - their fathers before them has lived its allotted span, it has grown old and devitalized. The temple is still there behind the imposing facade, but only the old men serve its crumbling altars; the unclean camp in its courts. Even as the priests intone the immortality of their gods, we feel that their day is over; already they are but names to us.

Meanwhile the people, the erstwhile congregation, drift to and fro in the streets, where the brazen-lunged showmen beat their big drums for this or that international cult, offers the unwary their cure-all nostrums, their cheap tickets for the millennium. We are puzzled, aimless, apprehensive.. Things are happening around us; sometimes they happen to us; but we do not know what they are or what they mean. The air is thick with contradictory rumours; the shouting is incessant. Many affirm that the "King is Dead," but few as yet shout, "Long Live the King."

Britain of the nineteen-thirties is trying for the last time the policy of "muddling through," which is interesting for the muddlers, but rather poor fun for those who have to foot the bill. So far flagrant opportunism has been able to postpone the day of decision. A series of diversions abroad has served to cloak the disruption within. The idea has been sedulously fostered that Britain is an island of stability in a sea of world unrest, that time will prove the wisdom of the static outlook, the virtue of immobility.

But not one of the three generations which make up the community can face the future with any confidence. The elders, the pre-War generation, are vaguely alarmed; their gods, it is true, are still in their niches, social respectability, class distinction, sound finance, international trade, are still officially revered. The average age of the Cabinet is still over 55 the gold reserves are imposing; the dialectic tourney at Westminster still runs its course; the monarchy has been purged and restored to docility. But they know that underneath the cairn surface currents are at work, undermining ancient foundations, shifting the old values. They prefer to look back, because they find it disquieting to look forward.

The War generation has suffered twenty years of anticlimax. Having escaped Hell, they have been denied that paradise which they felt was theirs by right of sacrifice; they have endured the purgatory of

THE WINTER OF OUR DISCONTENT

frustration and disillusionment. For four years they lived in a world of stark realism, with sudden death, physical pain and mental anguish as their constant companions; they returned to a world drifting steadily back to the old conventions, the time-honoured shams and deceptions, a world which had less and less use for them. One by one the banners under which they fought have followed their medals into the pawnshop; they feel that their sacrifice was in vain.

The post-War generation, because it has no past and has been given no future, lives frankly for the present. It dabbles, it experiments, as youth does and should, but with little satisfaction. Therefore it returns to the things of the moment, dress, speed, sport, and the unfailing fascination of "something for nothing" (or at any rate only a 6d. postal order). It is cynical, because there seems to be nothing in particular worthy of faith; it is materialistic, because there seem to be so few appeals to the spirit.

Therefore the birth-rate is falling, and the cinema is replacing the church as a cultural centre. Independence is at a discount, and there is an enormous demand for "safe jobs" which leave plenty of time and energy for pleasures of the moment. Why trouble to acquire skill, when everything will presently be done by machinery? Why be industrious when industry is patently ill-rewarded and the gambler everywhere fawned upon? Why plan for the future, when no one knows what the future will be like, save that it will probably be very nasty?

But few can find lasting satisfaction in cynicism and materialism. So the people are restless, impatient, seeking an outlet, a release from the grey meaningless routine of their lives, from the racket and strain of the economic dog-fight of the great cities. They flee at every opportunity to the country or the coast, dragging their nightmare with them. They drug themselves with the third-hand drama of the cinema, the radio, and the sensational Press. They gamble feverishly, incessantly, because a lucky bet seems the only way of escape. That is the motif of modern life — escape, escape, escape. Whence? Whither?

PART I

LIBERTY, EQUALITY, FRATERNITY!

The dominant political creed of the era which is now drawing to a close is Liberalism. Liberalism may be broadly defined as a belief that the first objective of human society should be the provision of the maximum degree of liberty, social, political and economic, for the individual. Its theory of government is, therefore, negative rather than positive; namely, that government should seek to facilitate the expression of individualism by protecting the individual from interference, rather than seek to lead, guide or control him in the furtherance of a common aim.

It follows that Liberalism tends to regard the nation, not as a corporate entity, but as a collection of individuals grouped together for certain limited mutual advantages. Although it has in the past been associated with subject races striving to throw off a foreign yoke, its general tendency is to deprecate any advance in positive nationalism as a form of restriction on the liberty of the individual. Hence it tends to be international rather than national in outlook, idealist rather than realist.

Historically, Liberalism dates from the French Revolution, its prophet was Jean Jacques Rousseau, its watchwords, Liberty, Equality, Fraternity, though a certain incompatibility between the first principle and the third has always tended to push the latter into the background

"All men are created free and equal." That was the keynote of the revolutionary spirit which swept Western Europe and the North American colonies a century and a half ago, which broke up Empires, destroyed dynasties and brought time-mellowed institutions crashing in ruins. For these words and all they were thought to express, men lived and died, and strove amid chaos and bloodshed to build new institutions free of the taint of servitude and restraint, of hereditary privilege and unequal justice.

LIBERTY, EQUALITY, FRATERNITY

That the revolution was successful is a matter of history, though the degree of success varied considerably from country to country. It succeeded because the crying need of the period was freedom of action and equality of opportunity. The old institutions had not merely been deflected from their original purposes by corruption and abuse, but were quite incompatible with the rapid advances of science and philosophy. With the improvement of communication, the rise of manufacturing industries, and the spread of literacy, systems based on the divine rights of monarchs and the political domination of a landed aristocracy could no longer command authority. They were anachronisms, and as anachronisms they were overthrown.

But in proportion, as the Liberal revolution succeeded, so it became itself the stronghold of vested interests dominated by a new hierarchy whose privileges were as great as those of the aristocracy which had fallen before the guillotine and the ballot-box. This process was all the more rapid because the principles of Liberalism are limited and negative. The problems of humanity are not solved by making all men free and equal, even in the restricted degree achieved by Liberalism; on the contrary, they are rendered the more complex, and new authorities spring up to replace those which have been overthrown. These new authorities can become in their turn just as tyrannical and oppressive as the old, in which case the principles for which the revolutionaries fought degenerate into meaningless catchwords, a soiled and tarnished cloak which hides the decay and, degradation of the revolution.

So it has proved with Liberalism. The very success of its revolt created a hiatus which was speedily occupied by new vested interests. As the political power of the aristocrat and courtier declined, it was taken over by the demagogue and the party politician. As the authority of the Churches declined, it has been taken over by the financial priesthood, maintaining what is virtually a materialistic form of religion, Money. The wheel has turned full circle.

In Britain the Liberal Revolution was comparatively slow and peaceful, but none the less effective. The Napoleonic wars, which were in no small measure an expression of British resistance to the new French Liberalism, accelerated deep-seated economic and social changes.[1] For a time the high price of commodities strengthened the power of the landed proprietor. But the rapid growth of public expenditure and debt tended to transfer this power to the financial and commercial classes, particularly when the war boom ended, as all war booms end, in a long and bitter period of deflation. The development of power manufacture was, at the same time, transferring population from the countryside to industrial towns.

Thus the Reform Act of 1832 was not so much an act of liberation as the political equivalent of social and economic changes which had already taken place. Nominally, power passed from the broad acres and rotten boroughs of the squirarchy to the teeming wens of the new industrial Britain. But these in turn became the instruments on which the hierarchy of the counting-house and cotton-mill could play the tune which served their interests best.

So the Liberal Revolution in Britain, though inspired by the same principles which produced it in France and undoubtedly the outcome of a popular movement, became in essence the charter of the bourgoisie, who found that the principles, of Liberty and Equality could be translated into terms of trade, industry and finance. With the Repeal of the Corn Laws and the Bank Charter Act, they at least achieved liberty. It is hardly surprising if they constitute the rear-guard of Liberalism.

This is not to say that the Liberal era must be written off as a failure. On the contrary, it marks an important phase in human development. The dynamic energy which it liberated carried the West far ahead of the rest .of the world. Nor is it necessary to dismiss the leaders of Liberalism as rogues and charlatans. On the contrary, many of them have been men of upright character, inspired with the earnestness of their mission. It would be but a poor tribute to them to cease building at the point where they laid down their task.

---

[1] There is an interesting parallel between Napoleon and Hitler. Napoleon the spearhead of liberalism, and Hitler, the spearhead of National Socialism.

THIS FREEDOM.

Since Liberty is always accorded first place among the attributes of Democracy; since Liberalism is, as its name implies, a creed based on Libertarian concepts; and since freedom is invariably emphasised by exponents of Democracy as the chief distinction between it and Fascism, it is pertinent to examine the theory of Liberty a little more fully than is usually the case among political writers and speakers. Should Liberty, for instance, be the chief objective of advancing civilisation? How much Liberty is allowed to the individual under the existing system? Is this Liberty of so much value to him that he should be prepared to make sacrifices in other directions in order to preserve it? Does it justify him in clinging to the existing system when other alternatives are presented to him? Do these alternatives involve a diminution in individual Liberty, and to what extent?

In the first place, it is obviously incorrect and misleading to refer to Liberty as an absolute condition; for in a civilised community complete freedom for the individual is quite impossible. The further we get from anarchy (which is after all the logical extreme of Liberalism), the more we must consent to restriction on Liberty; and on balance we usually consider it an advantage to exchange some measure of Liberty for a greater degree of security and a higher standard of living. If Liberty must thus be curbed and conditioned, is it wise to give it priority in the scale of political and social values?

In the second place, Liberty has negative rather than positive qualities; it implies the absence of evil rather than the existence of good. It is therefore not so much an end in itself as a means to an end. The Liberal Revolution was necessary in order to free Western man from his shackles; but if we do not use this freedom to build up a better world, we shall in a large measure be throwing away that which our forbears won for us.

In the third place, Liberty, in the absence of strong authoritarian government (which is the very antithesis of Liberalism), is apt to be very unevenly distributed. For the strong and the clever are free to obtain a larger share at the expense of the weak and simple. Particularly is this true in the economic sphere, in which millions are now just as much the slaves of the hooter and check-in clock, the foreman's whistle and the machine, as the medieval serfs were slaves of their feudal overlord.

It is true, of course, that the modern wage-earner can desert his tyrant in a way which was not open to the serf, but if he does not speedily enter the service of another tyrant he condemns himself and his family to hardship and misery. On the other hand, those who are able to derive a livelihood from invested capital, though by no means absolutely free, enjoy nevertheless relatively more liberty than those who have only their labour to sell.

A very large proportion of the community, in fact, is compelled to barter its freedom for the most elementary security from hunger and discomfort. And it is significant that most of the Liberty talk comes from the minority which has achieved this security, and these defenders of Liberty are not always wholly disinterested in their crusade.

Thus to the financier Liberty means freedom to move great blocks of capital about the world in search of bigger earnings, to buy and sell currencies and exploit political disturbances, to exact the highest rate of interest, which the needs of borrowers will stand. To the speculative trader it means freedom to buy in the cheapest market and sell in the dearest, to exploit human needs and human ignorance. To the press-magnate it means freedom to distort, exaggerate or suppress items of news in conformity with the policy of his publications, to promote rumours to the status of facts, to play upon human emotions as a means of selling his wares. To the politician it means freedom to employ national problems for party purposes, to obstruct useful legislation, to subordinate public service to his own career. To the intellectual it means freedom, if he so wishes, to distort truth and beauty, to disseminate false ideas, to undermine morality and patriotism.

These, and not the working population, are the modern devotees of Liberty, because it gives them licence to pursue their own ends without regard to the rights of others, because it enables them to set up a whole pantheon of their own, Money, Business, Art, Power and Party. While they demand from the nation their full share, and often more than their full share, of food, shelter, services and protections. Their first loyalty is not to the nation but to these gods of' their own, or to their own personal aggrandisement. It is these who dread the passing of a system which they have done so much to abuse, and bitterly oppose the rise of any system which imposes on them discipline and responsibility.

It is rather typical of this "Liberal Rearguard", which is seldom conspicuous for its patriotic scruples where money or careers are concerned, that it should strive to identify the love of Liberty as a peculiarly British characteristic. Particularly does it insist upon the Briton's attachment to political liberty, meaning, presumably, the mass-vote and so-called freedom of speech.

Now this is a clever perversion of the truth. The Briton, certainly, values personal liberty very highly; he resents any infringement upon it, and in particular the petty officialdom and fussy paternalism which seems inseparable from bureaucratic Socialism. But he perceives clearly enough that liberty must be tempered by justice, which, in fact, he ranks rather the higher of the two. Above all else, he resents being "put upon." And precisely because he is "put upon" by the present system, he makes such use as he can of the free speech which that system allows him as a safety-valve.

Thus he dislikes being made to stand in a queue, for it is, strictly speaking, a grave infraction of his civil right to free use of the public pavement; But because he acknowledges the justice of the principle of "first come, first served," and because the queue is the most practical means of upholding this principle, he does not object. Rather does he reserve his protests for the freedom-loving individual who seeks to elbow himself into a place in the queue to which he is not justly entitled.

Nor is it at all easy to believe that he derives as much satisfaction from the mass-vote as the party politicians would have us think. It is significant that he always refers to "the Government," not "our Government." And if the polling returns are any guide, he has much less faith in the democratic ballot-box than he has in that quite undemocratic institution, the hereditary monarchy.

After all, if democracy means party politics (which democrats will hardly deny), it also means governments, which are by no means fully representative of the nation. In point of fact, very few modern parliaments have been elected on a clear majority of total votes.

Thus democracy tends to produce minority governments, and if it does this it must also provide some compensation for the unrepresented. Seen in this light, Free Speech and the: right to criticise no longer appear as inestimable boons conferred, by democracy, but rather as concessions which render an imperfect system less intolerable. For it will hardly be contended that they are the best means of obtaining reforms, while the opportunities they provide for factionalism and obstructionism are obvious.

To take an industrial analogy: so long as managerial initiative is vested solely in employers, the employees must have a right to strike. But if a system can be built up whereby employees obtain a share in management, the strike weapon loses its value; it is in fact obsolete.

And so the Briton, being essentially a practical person, will in the long run assess political liberty at its real value to him, as measured in terms of social and economic justice. And for all that intellectual abstractionists may say, the democratic system is neither infallible nor eternal; nor is it even the best guarantee of personal liberty. -

DEMOCRACY IN THEORY AND PRACTICE

Democracy is the political expression of the Liberal ideal. It is itself an ideal, clear in principle, if nebulous in form, an ideal which inspired some of the greatest minds of the Liberal age. No one reading the famous Gettysburg oration can question Lincoln's sincerity of purpose or singleness of aim. "We here highly resolve that these dead shall not have died in vain, that this nation under God shall have a new birth of freedom and that the government of the people, by the people, for the people, shall not perish from the earth."

Yet so difficult is the theory of Democracy to translate into practice, so clumsy is it as a means of expressing the will of the people, that Lincoln himself, a few months prior to the Gettysburg dedication, was compelled to enforce military conscription in the face of bitter opposition in order to achieve the subjugation of another section of the American people. In fact, it is seriously open to question whether Lincoln at this period represented the majority of the, American people as a whole. While there is no doubt that he believed in the principles of democracy, he was able to establish them only by subordinating them to the genius of his personal leadership. Modern American democracy is hardly a fitting memorial to that genius, or to .the dead at Gettysburg.

But Democracy is full of paradoxes such as is this, and one is forced to the conclusion that Liberalism is altogether too narrow a view of human values on the one hand and political science on the other. Liberty and Equality are no more the sum total of man's ethical needs than the Democratic mass-vote is the last word in popular government. Instead of leading the nations of the West forward, step by step, Liberalism seems to have stopped short after its initial victories, making no attempt to show the liberated peoples how to use their newly-won rights, or how to develop the vote as a political instrument.

For democracy, shorn of all the trappings with which it has been loaded, means just this — that the will of the majority, as ascertained by a counting of heads, must prevail.

So crude a method as this, clearly cannot be regarded as more than a temporary and transitional stage. It may serve for a small primitive community, - though actually it is rarely found in such communities: it may serve for a small organisation formed for a specific purpose, though actually such organisations usually tend to follow the leadership of one or a few individuals.

But in a large and complex modern community, it is virtually impossible to ascertain the will of the people in this way, much less to translate it into action. The issues are many and highly technical. The registering of votes is a tedious and costly business. The information available to the general public is quite inadequate for them to form definite opinions, even when it is not distorted for propaganda purposes. Pure democracy — in the sense of government "by the people" — is a mere figment of the imagination.

So there has grown up a form of government, which is nominally democratic (and always referred to as such) but is actually a modified form of oligarchy, or government by the few. Many functions of government, especially those of an economic nature, have been removed altogether from popular control and are now the preserve of the financier and the bureaucrat. The residues are controlled by political groups and parties who, because they periodically resort to the mass vote, label themselves "representative."

The very term "representative" is misleading, if not positively inaccurate, since it conjures up visions of the inhabitants of a district, or the members of a trade or profession, choosing from among themselves the one who can best express their views and safeguard their interests. But under the existing system of pseudo-democracy, this is the exception rather than the rule. "Representatives" are first selected by political caucuses, and then put forward to solicit votes: consequently they represent the caucus rather than the voters. Initiative thus comes from above instead of from below, which is the very antithesis of Democratic principles.

It is perfectly true, of course, that anyone who can produce certain guarantees may stand for parliament, and that the voter may vote for any candidate. But the prospective legislator will find that in these days of intensive propaganda and political apathy the winning of a constituency entails so great an expenditure of time and money that in practice it can be hardly accomplished without the aid of party machinery. And if he should succeed in getting himself elected in defiance of powerful vested interests, he will find that parliamentary business is conducted almost entirely on party lines, so that while he may be able to pride himself on championing the lost cause of true Democracy, he is likely to find his legislative career singularly sterile.

The part played by the ordinary citizen in pseudo democratic politics is, therefore, purely nominal. He is in fact so much ballot-fodder. His choice of representatives is limited to the nominees of the parties, rarely more than three in number; indeed, if a wider choice were offered him, the system would become even more farcical than it is now, since it would be almost impossible to have a majority vote. He is quite unable to vote for any particular policy without at the same time voting for many other policies embodied in the party programme, some of which may be quite repugnant to him. He cannot, for instance, vote for the Labour policy of. coal nationalisation without voting for the whole gamut of International Socialism, including foreign policy. He cannot vote for Conservative tariffs without endorsing the Means Test.

It is quite true, of course, that as election-time approaches the political limelight is adroitly focussed on a single issue, which may or may not be the major problem of the moment, and may or may not be fairly presented to the public. But this is no guarantee whatever that a majority of votes obtained on this issue will result in effective action on the lines indicated by the election. Did the Labour government returned in 1929 "cure unemployment"? Did the National government returned in 1931 "save the pound"? Did the same government, when returned in 1935, "uphold the League Covenant"?

Judged by its own standards, Democracy as we know it today is an elaborate humbug: despite the fine ideals which inspired its earlier phases, it has failed lamentably as an instrument of popular government. It gives the people no freedom of choice; it does not reflect their will; it shamelessly betrays their confidence; it treats them with a contempt which is thinly veiled with resounding phrases. So discredited is it in the eyes of the people that it cannot even achieve its own first principle, a majority vote. It must be many years since any government received a clear mandate; even the "National" government of 1931, with its 10 to 1 majority in the House of Commons, polled a bare half of the total available votes (excluding those in unopposed constituencies). The present government holds office by virtue of 11¾ million votes out of 28 millions.

Yet this is the system to which Britain is supposed to be irrevocably wedded, the system which is said to represent the high-water-mark of political achievement, so sacrosanct that almost any kind of ineptitude may be perpetrated in its name, so precious to the British people that they must be prepared to lay down their lives in its defence. Is it really the principles of Democracy which they are asked to defend, or the political careerists to whom Democracy has become a vested interest?

PARTY POLITICS

If government under the pseudo-democratic system does not represent the people, and is not controlled by them, whom does it represent, and by whom is it controlled? The answer is undoubtedly to be found in the existence of a ruling class, a solid strata which exists between Throne and People, between electorate and executive, an oligarchy masquerading as the quintessence of democracy.

If anyone doubts the existence of this thing, let him study the attitude of the average citizen towards politics. John Smith is effectively cut off from active participation of the government of his own country, and despite the "political liberty" which is flung at his head every morning by the syndicated Press and every evening by the B.B.C., he is well aware of the fact. "Politics" are to him a thing apart, something he can watch from a distance with detachment or partisan enthusiasm according to his inclination; rather like professional football, but hardly so suitable for a quiet bet. He declines to accept responsibility for the course of events, and in many cases does not even trouble to record his vote on the occasions when it is solicited.

There is thus a considerable gap between government and the governed, and into this gap has crowded a host of professional politicians, propagandists, careerists, political theorists and organisers, flanked on the one hand by an entrenched Public Service, and on the other by an entrenched Plutocracy. Ostensibly this class is open to all, but actually it is the close preserve of those who say and do the right things, and take care to ingratiate themselves with the right people. Certainly it recruits from below, but only on the understanding that the recruits accept class discipline.

Ostensibly, too, this class plays the Democratic game, dividing itself into opposing factions, each of which claims to speak and act on behalf of public opinion. Indeed, so ingrained is the idea that political liberty necessarily involves factionalism that factionalism has become almost the sole expression of political liberty. So long as there is Government and Opposition, Socialism and Capitalism, the principle of "government of the people, for the people, by the people" is considered to be well and truly maintained.

In point of fact, this ruling class does very little positive ruling. It discusses and debates and harangues interminably, but the greater part of its legislative activity is dictated by external pressure. In the economic sphere it is at the mercy of financial interests; on technical matters it relies, having little knowledge of its own, on the Civil Service; it yields, more or less, to influential organisations. For electioneering purposes, of course, it must achieve a certain number of minor reforms, provided that these do not conflict with vested interests. For its chief obsession is its own preservation.

It should not be inferred, of course, that we are governed exclusively by unscrupulous and self-seeking persons. On the contrary, the political class includes many men and women of genuine public spirit, and if these occasionally seem to work chiefly for their own ends it may be because they genuinely believe these ends to be identical with the public interest.

But such good work as is done is achieved in spite of the system and not because of it. Just as the political class as a whole must concentrate on preserving itself, so each party within it must concentrate on defeating its opponents in the manipulation of the mass-vote, and at the same time take good care not to alienate powerful interests in the background. It is thus virtually impossible for any problem to be dealt with on its merits, not for lack of power, for a Prime Minister with a safe majority in the Commons can be a dictator if he wishes (and sometimes is), but because the line of approach is always that of compromise and expediency.

It is rather amusing to note how carefully the legend has been fostered that the party system is inseparable from Democratic government, if not indeed the finest expression of political liberty. As a matter of fact, it antedates democracy by several centuries. Conservatives and Liberals are the lineal descendants of the pre-Reform Tories and Whigs, which in their turn originated in rival Court parties of the absolute monarchy period. Though Conservatism, like Toryism, has usually been associated with the landed gentry and property-ownership, and Liberalism with trade and the professions, their differences in principle have ceased to be real. While it is the Liberal tradition to uphold the strict application of Liberal tenets, Conservatism has sought to adapt those tenets to the needs of the moment and the service of vested interests.

So though Liberalism has always tended to be purist, and Conservatism to be opportunist, actually the two parties are but rival factions of the same school of thought, paying lip-service to the same Democratic creed and serving the same financial masters. Hence there is no need to discuss Conservatism as a separate entity.

Even Socialism, though it began as a genuinely reformist movement, has surrendered to political convention and lost its revolutionary character. Indeed it might almost be said that the Liberal party on its deathbed has divided its stock-in-trade between Labour and Conservatism, so that the conventions of the two-party system may continue unimpaired. Thus the ideal of the modern pseudo-democrat is after all but a slight corruption of Gilbert's famous lines,
"Every little boy and girl that's born into this world alive.
Is either a little Labourite or - else Conservative."

And so democratic government of today is vested, not in the people, nor in leaders chosen by the people, but in the party. No matter how honest the intentions of the or how fine his ideals, he becomes, from the moment of his accepting nomination, the servant of the party, amenable to its discipline, pledged to uphold its policy regardless of his own personal convictions or the views of his constituents. Arrived at Westminster, he finds that Parliament is conveniently situated between the City and the West End, and in much closer touch with the continent of Europe than with the industrial and agricultural areas where the nation's wealth is produced and national problems await solution. Insensibly he absorbs the theatrical atmosphere of the sham-fight, and by the time he has graduated from chorus to a minor part he has become convinced that the farce is indeed real life.

It is significant that as soon as party government is called upon to exercise leadership, it appeals, not to the people in whose name it exercises its functions, but to its political opponents. Indeed it may be at some pains to keep the electorate in the dark until it has completed plans for its own preservation.

Thus the Labour party obtained office in 1929 on the grounds that the capitalist system was doomed and that Socialism must take its place. Its victory was the outcome of many decades of patient selfless work by rank-and-file Socialists. And yet as the event which they had prophesied and prayed for began to take shape, as the capitalist system rocked under shock after shock, the Macdonald government drew closer and closer to its opponents and ended by assisting in the salvage of the thing which it had been elected to abolish. It is true that as a minority government they would have been unable to adopt revolutionary measures, and that they were under heavy pressure from Finance, but in that case their obvious course as democrats was to appeal to the people for a decisive mandate, a course which they shirked shamelessly until the ground was cut from under their feet.

Similarly in 1936, a little clique of State, Church and Court officials interposed itself between the people and a popular young monarch who had always been held up to them as a model of "democratic royalty." Not only was the electorate not consulted, it was not even informed, until the situation was irretrievable. Though this was hailed as a triumph for democracy, it is significant that the Prime Minister responsible subsequently removed himself to a place where he was no longer required to face the electorate. Incidentally he nominated his own successor, who thus received his mandate neither from King nor people, but from the head of a party that enjoyed the confidence of less than half the electorate.

ECONOMIC LIBERALISM

Democracy is the political expression of Liberalism. Free Trade is its economic expression. For though the term has come to be applied specifically to external transactions, in Liberal philosophy it covers all economic transactions, including wages, prices, output, distribution and exchange. The same basic concepts are common to Democracy and Free Trade, the same emphasis on the liberty of the individual (or more accurately non-regulation), the same implicit belief that the various forces which make up modern society will automatically achieve equilibrium, the same tendency to deprecate leadership and encourage competition or factionalism.

The Liberal's faith in the collective wisdom of mankind in the mass is enormous. The lesson of mob-psychology seems to have been entirely lost upon him. Just as he relies upon a large, uninstructed electorate to throw up an efficient and representative government as a matter of course, so he relies upon a myriad of unregulated transactions to produce an efficient and equitable economic system. Such reasoning may be magnificent in its simplicity, but it is not sense, and it has in fact done great disservice to those whom Liberal leaders intended to benefit.

Democracy and Free Trade thus flowered side by side, products of a common stock. For the demagogue it was but an easy step from political freedom and the mass-vote to economic freedom and unregulated trade. It was not difficult to convince people emerging from the final stages of parochial feudalism, people who were just beginning to realise the possibilities of cheap and rapid communications, that restraint in any form was contrary to the inalienable rights of man. It was not difficult to persuade the landless peasant and the workless craftsman, as they were drawn irresistibly into the machine of industrialism, what an immense- boon it was to them to be able to sell their labour in the dearest market and buy their necessities in the cheapest.

The Liberal Revolution, as we have seen, was essentially a transfer of power from the landed aristocracy to the bourgeoisie, from the nobleman and squire to the banker, merchant and mill-owner. The common people, in whose name the Revolution was made, were never more, and have never been more, than pawns, so many votes, and so many units of labour. But there can be no disguising the fact that the transition, sordid though it was in many of its aspects, was enveloped in an aurora of perfectly genuine enthusiasm for abstract ideals, almost religious in its intensity.

The fervour with which Nonconformity denounced the narrowness and ritualism of the Established Church, and the fervour with which Democracy denounced the corruption and inefficiency of rotten-borough parliaments, overflowed into the economic field until the doctrine of Free Trade became invested with the halo of crusade.

The "law of supply and demand" seemed the heaven-sent formula for justifying the boundless possibilities of commercial expansion in the new era of steam-power. The principle of "enlightened self-interest" seemed to prove beyond any shadow of doubt that since no man could enrich himself without enriching his fellow's unrestricted enterprise had full moral sanction and any form of regulation was a clear contravention of natural laws. If imported corn could be sold for less than the cost at which corn could be grown at home, was it morally wrong to keep it out? If children could earn a few shillings a week in the mills, was it was morally wrong to deny them employment? If savages desired European firearms for the furtherance of tribal massacres, was it morally wrong to forbid such trade? The cloak of Liberty was flung wide.

But the British sense of justice has never been atrophied entirely, and it soon became evident that many things sanctioned by the economic "laws" of Free Trade were in fact incompatible with humanitarian principles. And it was not long before the process of humanising internal Free Trade was begun, especially in regard to labour conditions, a process which has continued down to the present day. External Free Trade resisted much more effectively, partly because of the powerful interests which have come to be associated with it, partly because its principal victim, agriculture, could readily be confused in

ECONOMIC LIBERALISM

the public mind with unpopular landlordism, partly because people could not see, and were not told of, the conditions under which imported goods were produced. Even now external Free Trade has been modified only in a tentative and highly discriminatory manner.

Liberalism was thus in a dilemma. It could, and did, resist the earlier modifications of its "economic laws," but when it became evident that the modification process was likely to continue it had to devise some formula whereby the prestige of those laws could be maintained even when their strict application was no longer permitted. Its solution was the elevation of its economic theory to the status of an exact science, divorced from unscientific affairs like politics and sociology, a science which acknowledges no authority but its own laws, and which politicians and social reformers defy at their peril.

Thus it is held to be "uneconomic" to produce oil from our own coal, even though we have many neglected coal-seams, thousands of unemployed miners, and an enormous home market for oil. It is held to be "uneconomic" to put displaced export-workers on the land, where they could grow the food which they can no longer earn by their former occupations. The so-called science of economics has, in fact, ceased to operate in terms of realities, such as men, commodities and resources, but only through the medium of an artificial money-standard, as interpreted by those who control the money system. The ordinary businessman is on sounder ground when he asserts bluntly that "Business is Business"; he may use the phrase to justify anti-social or unpatriotic actions, but at least he does not pretend to be scientific.

And so economic Liberalism or Free Trade has been just as successful as political Liberalism or Democracy in demonstrating an important truth. This truth is that Liberty and quality are not in themselves adequate bases for modern society, and are in fact, if emphasised to the exclusion of other considerations, mutually destructive. Economic liberty implies that the clever and greedy are free to exploit the simple and honest, and eventually reduce them to bondage and conditions of inequality. Perhaps worst of all, in its blind belief in self-interest as motive power, in its insistence on a theory of automatic self-regulation and equilibrium, it has created a demon un-amenable to codes of equity and morality, a demon on whose shoulders the incompetent politician and unscrupulous financier can lay responsibilities that they are glad to shirk.

THE GREAT TRADE MYTH

Trade is not one of the essential activities of man. Production obviously is essential; so also in any society but the very primitive is the barter or exchange of goods. But the main object of production is consumption, not trade; nor is barter necessarily trade. Trade is basically an artificial creation, the art of exploiting variations in the supply of goods and the demand for them as translated into money prices. And the fact that the trader has to perform certain useful services is by no means proof that he is indispensable. He may indeed become parasitic, and the recurrent outcry against dealers, speculators and middlemen does not arise entirely from prejudice.

It is clear that as society develops and the processes of barter become more complicated, the trader comes to occupy an extremely strong position. His greater intimacy with market conditions and his quicker turnover of money capital, enable him to dictate terms to producers, and to a large extent to consumers also. While he cannot directly control production, he can manipulate prices: and the fact that the majority of producers, being debtors, are forced sellers gives him a tremendous advantage.

This strategic position of the trader has always been recognised and until comparatively modern times elaborate precautions were taken by monarchs and other authorities to ensure that it was not used unfairly. Indeed the restrictions laid upon traders sometimes amounted to persecution. But these restrictions were already relaxing by the time that the Liberal Revolution took shape, and with the triumph of Liberalism came the complete emancipation of trade.

Once freed from his shackles, the trader rapidly became the central figure in the economic situation. The rapid increase in industrial production provided him with ample material; improved transport and communications facilitated his transactions; the opening up of new countries overseas provided immense opportunities; the money system was adapted to his advantage. It is significant that Liberalism gave its economic system the title of "Free TRADE".

Now fundamentally trade is not an end in itself, but only a means to an end. In so far as it adjusts supply and demand, and moves goods to where they are required, it is of value to the community. But any activity over and above this simply widens the gap between production and consumption, and by introducing further intermediate charges reduces the price which the producer receives and increases the price which the consumer must pay. It is in fact perfectly possible to have too much trade.

But Liberalism, because it believed that its competitive system would automatically cut down costs and check exploitation, could see in trade only the efficient functioning of the economic machine. In its eyes all trade was good trade, and the more the better. Industries did not exist in order to supply the needs of the people, but in order to make "trade", and because foreign trade involved more transactions and allowed more wealth to flow through the channels of commerce, it was much to be preferred to domestic trade, which might in certain circumstances hardly be called trade at all.

This was not of course the only attraction of foreign trade. The key to trade profits is the variable price, and international variations in price are usually much greater than variations within national boundaries. These variations were particularly advantageous to the British trader during the 19th century because our early start in industrial development had given us a long lead over other nations, and our manufactured goods could command almost monopoly prices in the new and backward countries which were then being opened up for trade. These prices, when translated into terms of primary commodities, represented substantial profits, - quite apart from the pickings incidental to international trade.

Behind the purely commercial aspects of foreign trade lay the financial aspects. Industrial profits, to say nothing of speculative profits, were piling up. To what better purpose could they be put than the making of loans to customer countries, which loans of course were exported in the form of manufactured goods, thus creating more profits for industry? To a large extent the same end could have been served by distributing the profits in the form of higher wages and thus increasing domestic purchasing power. But apart from the fact that the local customer does not make the same amount of business for trade intermediaries as does the foreign customer, it would have been considered grossly "uneconomic" to pay a higher rate of wages than that set "naturally" by the pressure of population and the pangs of hunger.

Therefore foreign trade became the be-all and end-all of this Golden Age of Liberal capitalism. And because those interested commercially or financially in foreign trade have ever since exercised an influence out of all proportion to their numbers, foreign trade is still the obsession of our ruling class regardless of their political allegiance.

As a direct result, we have had fastened on us certain time-honoured fallacies which are by now sadly in need of debunking.

(i) Trade (i.e., dealing in goods and moving them about) is the main economic objective, and the volume, of trade is a measure of economic efficiency.

(ii) Foreign trade, including the export of goods which we can consume at home in order to be able to import goods which we can produce at home, is therefore to be preferred to home trade.

(iii) Britain is an "industrial" country. i.e., the excess of manufacturing capacity developed during the brief and abnormal period of export activity must for evermore be supported by the community and determine the basis of economic policy.

(iv) "We cannot feed ourselves", i.e., because we have neglected our land for upwards of half a century we must on no account attempt to restore its natural functions.

(v) "We cannot live by taking in one another's washing". This, if it means anything at all, is simply a re-statement of (ii).

(vi) The revival of international trade is essential to world peace, i.e., nations can be friendly only with those with whom they do business, money presumably being thicker than blood. International debts and competition for markets are also extremely effective in promoting sympathetic relations.

To this gallery of Free Trade masterpieces must be added that unique achievement of the Liberal mind, the consumer complex. This complex can best be summarised as a belief that the deciding factor in production and distribution must always be the ultimate purchaser of goods and services and the money-price which be is willing to pay; to this factor all other factors must be subordinated. This was in the first place no doubt a literal interpretation of Adam Smith's highly dogmatic and rather questionable assertion that "consumption is the sole end and purpose of all production." At any rate, "the consumer" has served admirably as a moral justification for the barbarities of the competitive system.

The truth of the matter is that Man, like the beasts of the field, is a consuming animal, but, unlike the beasts of the field, he is also a creative animal, and the dynamic urge of the creative instinct is one of the mainsprings of civilisation. Thus the consumer complex is a hopelessly one-sided and inadequate concept of human activity. In point of fact, a truly civilised community does not produce solely for purposes of consumption, but devotes its surplus energies to production which cannot by any stretch of the imagination be called "consumable goods." Instead of perpetuating unemployment as a national institution, or alternatively theorising about the advantages of "leisure," it creates cathedrals, parks and national monuments.

In a fully-planned economy, with every legitimate interest safeguarded, it is, of course, quite possible to approach all economic problems from the viewpoint of use (which is a better term than "consumption"). A concept of this nature is, in fact, general in Socialist circles; it is logical, if materialistic.

But in a Free Trade economy, with a ruthless competitive system at full blast, its unjust action has produced a corresponding reaction.

In short, the formula which was designed to justify the competitive principle has come near to abolishing it altogether. For trade unionism on the one hand and monopolistic capitalism on the other, are, in sober truth, the inevitable consequences of Free Trade.

Apart from its questionable reasoning, the consumer-complex perpetrates a glaring injustice in that it always tends to penalise productive consumers in favour of unproductive consumers. It is claimed, for instance, that the competitive system, by continually forcing prices downwards, increases the purchasing power of consumers. But those consumers who depend for their livelihood upon the processes of production lose in lower wages and profits a large proportion of what they gain in lower prices, while those consumers whose incomes are not directly related to the processes of production (such as rentiers, pensioners and many Civil Servants) derive a clear gain which they have never earned.

Further objections are (i) that every fall in prices proportionately increases overhead costs (especially fixed interest charges), thus leaving a smaller residue to be distributed in wages and profits; (ii) that the system produces a permanent condition of flux and insecurity; and (iii) that if genuine (as distinct from forced) economies are effected in production, the benefit should accrue to those who have brought about the increased efficiency, i.e., the producers. At the present time, "efficiency" is apt to be the carrot dangled just in front of the donkey's nose.

THE FRUITS OF FREE TRADE

Britain has now had almost a century of Free Trade, for although some of the more obvious and less endurable faults of the system have perforce been modified, its theories are still embodied in official economic policy, just as the theory of democracy is still embodied in the system of government. It seems worthwhile therefore to refer to the effects which it has had on national life and economy.

(i) It has created a fantastic mal-distribution of wealth, which in turn has produced class hostility and a spirit of resentment which hampers and distorts genuine reformist effort. Misused Liberty has indeed destroyed Equality, and it is significant that most equalitarian theorists now base their classless society on the property-less mass, i e , the proletariat.

(ii) It has created a powerful and wealthy class of merchants and financiers, i.e., free traders in goods and money, which class has for some time past been engaged in liquidating its weaker members with a view to entrenching itself in monopolies.

(iii) It has created a vested interest of obsolete economic theory, which interprets the new only in terms of the old and is therefore essentially reactionary.

(iv) By favouring trade at the expense of production it has tended to reduce the proportion of producers in the able.-bodied population and thus slow down the creation of real wealth.

(v.) It has tended to concentrate population at those points where profits are most easily made and has thus created the vast, shapeless and often unwholesome wens, congested with the traffic of human activity, in which three-quarters of our people now live in utterly unnatural surroundings.

(vi) This process of urbanisation, plus unhealthy and uninspiring working conditions, plus a diet consisting overmuch of stale processed food, has played havoc with national health and resulted in the widespread use of unnatural palliatives

(vii) It has created a hopelessly lopsided economy, which produces an embarrassing surplus of certain types of wealth, and an alarming deficiency of other types. External markets have to be found for the former, and external suppliers for the latter, thus rendering a population of 46 millions utterly dependent on world conditions which they cannot control and are in fact highly unstable.

(viii) This dependence has in turn created a vicious circle which penalises all except those traders and financiers who are in a position to exploit it. Cheap exports necessitate cheap labour, cheap labour necessitates cheap living, cheap living necessitates cheap imports, cheap imports necessitate cheap exports. So long as we must compete overseas with other races (and in particular ultra-cheap Asiatic labour), this vicious circle is a standing menace to our standard of living.

(ix) Export economy has resulted in a huge network of international mortgages, which has proved so intolerable that it is now in process of being liquidated. At the same time, the tribute extorted by this mortgage system has displaced much home production,, and made us dependent upon supplies which must sooner or later dry up.

(x) Urbanisation, plus the vicious circle of external trade, plus the tribute imports of the mortgage system, has checked the natural development of our own agriculture and resulted in a criminal waste of natural resources. Thus the one major industry which could (a) right our lop-sided economy by absorbing surplus manufactures and employing displaced export workers; (b) remove our deplorable, dependence of world markets for essential foodstuffs, and (c) place the national diet on a sounder basis, which has been ruthlessly sacrificed for the temporary advantage of those who were able to exploit Free Trade.

(xi) This distorted economy has been propped up, and its inevitable poverty and unemployment relieved, by capital construction on a grand scale. This capital construction, e.g., houses, shops and offices, roads and armaments, would be in the main desirable if financed out of income. But financed as it has been by inflating still further an already oppressive debt system, it is merely postponing the day of reckoning. Moreover comparatively little of it will stimulate the future production of real wealth.

So this then is the Britain which a century of Free Trade has created, a Britain which, though nominally free, is in all essentials utterly dependent on the willingness of other nations to obey the dictates of our economic and financial system. And since these other nations are rapidly developing economic systems of their own, and are approaching the day when they will demand financial independence (or at least drastic adjustment), our position will become not only increasingly humiliating, but increasingly untenable.

The world is no longer amenable to, the old Liberal concept of "industrial" countries interchanging their products with "agricultural" countries, a concept which was at best an oversimplified interpretation of purely temporary phenomena. Every "industrial" country except Britain has seen the wisdom of building up its own agriculture to counterbalance manufacturing development. Every "agricultural" country is engaged in building up its own manufacturing industries. International trade may or may not be all that its exponents claim for it, but it certainly is not a game which we can play by ourselves.

One of the hardest lessons which the British business man has had to learn, and which he has still imperfectly digested, is that you cannot eat your cake and have it too.

You cannot equip countries twice over; nor, having sold them machinery, can you continue to sell them the products of similar, and perhaps less up-to-date, machinery; nor, having extolled the benefits of industrialisation, can you -expect others not to follow your example. The sun may have stood still for Joshua, but the sun of world trade will not turn back on its tracks for the benefit of export-capitalism. An adverse trade balance of £450 millions is the writing on the wall.

THE FRUITS OF FREE TRADE

Some forms of external exchange will, of course, always be necessary. A sound Imperial policy would give us an assured supply of tropical products in exchange for surplus manufactures. But such exchange will be complementary in character, barter rather than trade, with the self-destructive debt element avoided as far as possible. The policy of trade for trade's sake, of reducing weaker economic units to financial vassalage, is fast approaching its logical conclusion.

Why then are all the efforts of democratic governments, as well as those of financial hierarchy, directed to "reviving" international trade? Why do our leading politicians, bankers, economists and captains of industry so insist that we cannot live on our own resources? Why are exports regarded as a measure of efficiency and imports as a measure of prosperity?

It is true that there have been some hesitant fumbling with the concept of autarchy, or economic independence. The currency is less rigidly fastened to gold: certain powerful industries have effective protection; others less powerful have nominal protection; there has been some petty .byplay with import-quotas and organised marketing; and wherever wage-earners have organised in sufficient strength they have checked the worst abuses of free trade in labour. Yet it is perfectly clear to anyone who studies the utterances of bank chairmen, managing directors, and Ministers of the Crown that these concessions are regarded, for the most part as temporary expedients dictated by the shortcomings of other nations, to be abandoned as soon as it becomes possible to return to that Golden Age of Victorian Liberal capitalism in which orthodox economic thought is still centred.

There are perhaps two reasons. The first is that almost without exception our rulers and advisers were brought up in the Liberal Free Trade atmosphere and instinctively adhere to its traditions. For the most part they are past the age at which old ideas can be discarded and new ideas developed. Hence, it is folly to expect a new system to be worked out by those who owe their position to the old system.

Leaders who look backwards are not likely to take us very far: and with the downward swing of the pendulum now developing, it is no longer a question of whether the old economic order can be preserved but of what system is to replace it.

The second reason is less obvious, goes deeper, and is much harder to analyse. It is for that very reason likely to be the more important of the two. It is discussed in the following chapter.

FINANCIAL DICTATORSHIP

When Liberalism established freedom of trade in goods and money, and thereby abdicated any semblance of economic control by representatives of the people, it was clearly acting on the supposition that natural "laws" of equilibrium would operate to produce a self-regulating economy. This supposition has since proved invalid. There is probably no such thing as a self-regulating economy, any more than there is such a thing as a self-expressing public opinion. The question then arises: who or what has acquired the control (or at least influence) which the Liberals abdicated.

The clue surely is to be found in Money. In the absence of authority, the Money Standard has become supreme, and has, as we have seen, ousted all other standards over a wide range "of activities. "Business is Business", "Money talks", and so on. And since Money is no more self regulating than any other part of the economy, it follows that those who control the Money system control in effect the whole national situation. This unseen, non-representative power, which is in fact a dictatorship, is usually and most conveniently referred to as Finance.

Now it is undeniable that every civilised community requires an efficient Money system. Money has two important services to render. First, it must be an acceptable and freely-available medium of exchange; and second, it must be a stable measure of value. But if Money itself acquires value, and furthermore a variable value (in terms of all other things); if it is restricted in quantity in order that its value may be manipulated, then it ceases to be a freely-available medium of exchange or a stable measure of value. It ceases to be a servant and becomes the master. A good deal of confusion seems to have arisen among Socialists through the generalised use of the term "profit-motive" because there are clearly two kinds of profit. Profits earned by the production of real wealth or by the rendering of useful services, may or may not be excessive, may or may not have been acquired in antisocial ways, but at least they represent real value, which value, is only measured in terms of Money. But profits made out of

Money itself by buying and selling currencies, by hiring out fixed sums at interest or usury (there is no real distinction), or by exploiting the variable value of Money (i.e., price fluctuations) is essentially immoral, because no value is given in exchange.

Money-breeding or Money-dealing is, in fact, prostitution of common property, and one of the most damning indictments of Social-Democracy is the fact that it makes little or no attempt to cope with this, the greatest evil of financial capitalism. It is significant that the only recorded occasion on which Christ used violence is when he overthrew the tables of the Money-changers, and that the Church for many centuries forbade the practice of usury to Christians.

If it was necessary that this tremendous power should be concentrated in the Money system, the only way in which it could equitably have been administered would have been through the elected representatives of the people. But though modem governments can, and sometimes do, influence monetary policy, and not always in the interests of, the people, the real power rests with those who operate the system itself. And because Finance works internationally as well as nationally it is able not only to dictate the conditions under which people earn their livelihood, but to uphold or destroy any government which the people elect, unless and until that government takes steps to restore to the people the power which they have lost.

The better to consolidate its position, Finance has built around the money system a screen of technical complexities, so that the public have come to regard it in much the same way as a primitive tribe regards its witch-doctor, something mysterious and unintelligible, to be feared and placated rather than understood and criticised. In particular there are two superstitions or misconceptions which vitiate any intelligent appreciation of economic problems. One is that the supply of Money is physically limited the other is that Money has a fixed intrinsic value.

It is true, of course, that so long as gold remains the nominal basis of the currency, the volume of currency in circulation has arbitrary limits; which is an excellent argument for a non-gold currency. But credits, which are created by book entry, exceed by many times the tangible currency, and are virtually limited only by considerations of policy.

Again, Money varies in value according to the amount of commodities which it will buy. Price fluctuations are not due to variations in the intrinsic value of commodities, which, broadly speaking tends to remain constant, but to variations in the purchasing-power of Money. These in turn are due for the most part to variations in the ratio between the volume of goods available for purchase and the volume of money available for making purchases.

It is through these two illusions, namely limited supply and fixed value, that Finance exercises the greater part of its power. The first illusion enables it to scare up the necessary popular support when it seeks to attack a "spend-thrift" or "uneconomic" policy, or when it needs an "economy campaign" for the easier adjustment of its own excesses. More important still, it provides sanction for the charging of interest or hire for the use of credit. A great many people, of course, who cannot by any stretch of imagination be called financiers, derive income from interest. But these are secondary creditors, re-lending money which has already paid interest at the source. The primary creditor is the financial system, because it has a monopoly in the original issue of credit.

It is this interest principle, which makes the debt system so iniquitous, for the temporary transfer of purchasing power is not in itself vicious. But the fact that money cannot be "made," according to the popular idea, out of production and trade, means that interest can be paid only by fresh borrowing. Thus a debt of £100 at 5% automatically involves in the repayment of £200 by the end of twenty years. Certainly the original borrower may have cleared himself by obtaining the interest from others, or by passing on the obligation. But the community as a whole is liable for this steadily increasing burden of debt. The situation can be relieved only by the transfer of real wealth (e.g., land or equipment) to the financial institutions, or by some upheaval sufficiently violent to cause the writing-off of debts as irrecoverable.

This process would be bad enough if £100 remained the same sort of £100 throughout the twenty-year period, but money of variable value means that the £ is constantly fluctuating in terms of the things which it will buy. Thus a farmer who borrows £100 at a time when each £ is worth a sack of wheat may find in a few years' time that a £ is worth two sacks, so that he has to pay ten sacks a year in interest at 5%, and is liable for the repayment of 200 sacks.

These fluctuations may, of course, operate against creditors as well as against debtors, particularly in cases where Money loses value rapidly as the result of inflationary finance. But, generally speaking, credit is issued most abundantly during "boom" periods when commodity prices are high and the value of money is low, so that the subsequent downward trend of prices and upward trend - of Money value inflates debts and enslaves debtors.

In fact, to a very large extent, so-called trade cycles are basically financial debt cycles. During a boom credit is freely available, and is borrowed on a large scale for purposes of production. But it is also borrowed for speculative purposes, and when speculation has forced capital values up to dangerous levels, the financial' system is forced to initiate a policy of credit-withdrawal or deflation, which creates an atmosphere of depression, and perhaps panic. Capital values fall abruptly and with them commodity prices, for the contraction of profits and wages restricts purchasing power. Debts are automatically inflated, and debtor producers are compelled to sell at any sacrifice, thus forcing prices lower still until the bottom of the slump is reached. At this point debts are either written off or liquidated by the transfer of real property, and many producers as well as speculators become unemployed or bankrupt. Then as the clearance of stocks steadies prices, and unused credits begin to accumulate in the financial system, the latter begins to lend freely again, and the debt system re-expands.[2]

---

2 The Right Hon. B. Mc:Kenna (Chairman) In an address - to Midland Bank shareholders: January 26th, 1938: "The year 1937 opened with a good prospect of sustained business improvement. The industrial outlook was so promising, indeed, that fears were expressed of a coming boom. There were signs of growing speculation on the Stock Exchange

FINANCIAL DICTATORSHIP

But the second, illusion, that of fixed money value, prevents the community from perceiving the true nature of its economic discomforts. It tries to remedy the effects (unstable prices) instead of removing the cause (unstable money). It demands new credits (an increase in debt) instead of reforming the debt system. It tries to reduce costs and promote efficiency by "saving labour" instead of putting more purchasing power into circulation through wages.

Thus Financial Dictatorship is constantly breaking down, because Finance is essentially parasitic on production, and whenever producers are weakened and handicapped, Finance itself becomes deranged. But with each successive crisis the parasite draws strength from the host and acquires a firmer grip. The growth of great combines is a sure indication that the control of production and trade is passing into the hands of those who manipulate great blocks of Money capital. i.e., Finance.

The most menacing feature of a menacing situation is the fact that Finance is operated internationally by men of frankly cosmopolitan outlook. By transferring capital, it can thus play off one section of producers against another, forcing down wages by dumping the products of sweated labour in another country. By manipulating the exchanges it can virtually blackmail national governments into sanctioning its activities. By usurping economic power it has reduced representative governments to a mere shadow-show and created a dictatorship of the worst possible type.

---

and in raw materials; some commodities, especially metals made a disturbing jump. Speculation, however, was speedily checked by a reduction in the quantity of money, and a decline in prices followed."

SPRING COMES AGAIN

THE PLUTOCRATIC STATE

The final stage of any era is almost invariably characterised by degeneration and corruption, and Liberalism is no exception. Of the high ideals which inspired the Liberal Revolution little remains but the mass-vote, and even this is exploited shamelessly for party purposes by the oligarchy which has constituted itself the guardian of democracy.

This oligarchy in turn is but the political instrument, as the Money system is the economic instrument, of a dictatorship which is certainly not of the people and does not even pretend to represent them. In view of the existence of this dictatorship, in view of the tacit acceptance of the Money standard, the use of the Stock Exchange (or more accurately Debt Exchange) as an economic barometer, the predominance of the rich in the ruling class, the key-position accorded to the Treasury in the governmental structure, and the deference paid to the City, it would be inaccurate to classify the system by which Britain is now governed as anything but plutocracy.

Everywhere are the signs of the Money cult. Plutocracy, accepting no values but its own Money standard, is frankly and blatantly materialistic. Therefore the dominant note today is one of unashamed vulgarity. Not the homely, bawdy vulgarity of the pothouse and barrack-room, but the synthetic self-advertising vulgarity of the nightclub and the lido, a vulgarity which applauds the monstrosities of Epstein and the Surrealists as Art, which buys publicity by the yard, which believes that everything can be reduced to terms of Money. We have exercised the crusty cob-webby devil of Privilege, only to let in the seven sleek chromium-plated devils of Plutocracy.

Our Plutocracy, unlike many of its more ostentatious members, is no parvenu; its growth has been contemporaneous with that of its Liberal host. Go back to Cobbett, and you will find in his stock-jobbers and fund-holders the very prototypes of the smooth marcelled crew who now dominate the West End and monopolise the more expensive pleasure resorts. Even then the Brighton road was being improved so

THE PLUTOCRATIC STATE

that the Money-spinners might sleep and keep their women by the sea while they courted Mammon in the City.

For the plutocrats of that time had battened on the Napoleonic wars, even as the profiteers did a century later on another Great War, waxing fat on government contracts and public debt. Then, despoiling the old land-owning class of their corn profits, they became the mortgagees of Britain as well as the creditors of the State. And the fruits of the industrial revolution fell into their laps like ripe plums

At first the rising manufactures were the work of small producer capitalists. But with the introduction of larger units of machinery, and the need for wider markets, came the necessity for larger units of production. The producer capitalist had perforce to enlist the services of the finance capitalist, or became one himself. Company promotion became a recognised profession. Power passed from the masters of machinery and organisers of labour to the masters of Money and organisers of Big Business. Industry became impersonalised, a giant inhuman machine. And the process of financial conquest was begun which is now ending in monopoly of production and distribution.

While trustification was proceeding at the top, demoralisation was setting in at the bottom. Industrialisation, of course, has always had certain material advantages to offer in the way of cheap goods; but they have been dearly bought. The craftsman, after all, can offer some measure of resistance to the monopolist. His craft gives him moral strength and economic bargaining power; it educates his hands and mind. But the machine-minder is simply a human unit; he can be taught his little routine in a few hours, and replaced in as short a time from the ranks of the workless, which unregulated industrialisation creates. The very machines which he tends can be used to drive him quite as effectively as any slave-whip.

Divorced from the soil, unsupported by craftsmanship, he becomes in effect the slave of the system which employs him and to which he must look for foods, housing, warmth, even entertainment and information. Dazzled by the illusion of political freedom, the working man has blundered headlong into the web of economic serfdom, and not a few of those whom he has trusted to fight his battles have simply used his shoulders as a ladder wherewith to attain their own ease and security.

To some extent the small capitalist has contrived to resist the advance of financial monopoly. The individual manufacturer, the small trader and the farmer are not yet completely submerged. Battered from below by resentful Labour, squeezed from above by ruthless Finance, pin-pricked on every side by arrogant bureaucracy, they have a desperate struggle to keep their foothold. But because they are the great intermediate element, which can provide the ambitious wage-earner with a chance to achieve some measure of independence, because they can furnish the real leaders of industry and commerce, and because, they are the, great stabilising factor in any society, they must be an essential part of the regenerated nation.

There could be no better testimony to the degeneration of democracy than the extent to which - the plutocrat is prepared to use his vast resources in its defence. Democracy, as practised today, serves his purpose better than anything that he could have devised himself. It presents him with a flock of sheep, a leaderless mob which can be mustered and driven by his working dogs, the Parties and the Press, and brought in due course to the shearing-board. Anything, which converts the mob into a coherent unit under effective leadership, challenges his power. Therefore the whole of the Money interest, from the titled City magnate to the petty slum usurer, is an implacable opponent of Fascism and National Socialism.

Britain of the nineteen-thirties is being moulded, subtly but remorselessly, into a docile proletariat, a vassal state of International Finance. Democracy has produced no leaders to oppose Finance, but only misleaders, men who dare not treat the people as intelligent beings who can be told the truth. Hence the smoke-screen of empty verbiage, the sloganised party war-cries and the cheap sensation mongering of the trustified Press. Hence a shiftless, temporising foreign policy, for ever trying to bluff its way out of untenable positions and feigning righteous indignation when its bluff is called. Hence the fatuity of trying to deal with dynamic realities in terms of static formula.

But the British are a stubborn race, slow to anger, not easily convinced, not easily bribed. Enslaved by Finance, bemused by commercialised propaganda, drugged by cheap Jewish entertainment, confronted almost daily with so-called crises which are none of their making, they nevertheless retain a true appreciation of right and wrong. Even as they know that the forces which control Britain today are "all wrong," so they know that Britain herself is still "all right." In their deep, inarticulate belief in their own country they possess reserves of strength and independence - which neither organised Plutocracy nor organised Communism can altogether destroy. Though the winter has been long and drear, they know that Spring will come.

PART II - THE AGE OF FORMULAE

THE ENDLESS QUEST

LIBERTY, as we have seen, is a gravely inadequate basis for the political and economic structure of a civilised community. Indeed, the logical end of increasing Liberty is Anarchy, and wherever the Anarchist movement has appeared as in Spain, it has always been attributable to the impact of Liberalist doctrines upon people who have not yet learnt the limitations of Liberty as a political creed. Authority is inseparable from civilisation.

Now authority may take one of two forms, personal or aristocratic leadership, or a series of formula embodied in laws and conventions. Leadership may be good, bad or indifferent; it may carry a nation to the heights or, plunge it into misery; it may or may not command the willing co-operation of the led; but at least it gets results. It is the dynamic form of authority.

Formulae, equally, may be good or bad, but in most cases they are indifferent, because, being essentially static and inflexible, they cannot be adapted to the ever changing currents of national life. However carefully and wisely they are devised, however often they are revised, they must have a restrictive effect on growth and development. By their very nature they represent an attempt to legislate for the future in terms of the past; and when there occurs some unforeseen event which calls for rapid adjustment, their effect may be disastrous. In any case, they set a premium on age, conservatism and timidity, and offer a happy hunting ground for vested interests. Per contra, they set a discount on youth, courage and vigour, and tend to obstruct the will of the people.

This is not to say that formulae are necessarily undesirable. On the contrary, every civilised community has uses for formulae, for laws and regulations of various kinds. But as soon as it ceases to regard these formulae as its servants, - and allows them to become a vested interest, it surrenders its natural rights and abandons forward movement: for there are very few formulae which will stand the test of time.

Liberalism, in its early, dynamic stages, was essentially a revolt from formulae, such as the divine right of kings and the theory of hereditary nobility. By the same token, it owed much to leadership (e.g., Napoleon). But in adopting democracy as its political interpretation, and the party system as the machinery of democracy, it put leadership at a discount. For the very fact that a statesman is acknowledged the leader of one party automatically disqualifies him for the support of other parties, and no matter what his gifts, denies him the status of national leadership. Democracy is ever distrustful of greatness.

So, Liberal democracy has become more and more a thing of formulae, dissipating its energies in search of yet more formulae, and losing its original dynamic urge at every step. Even poor Lincoln, essentially a leader, will be remembered chiefly for his historic formula for democracy; a good thing of its kind, certainly, but still a formula. Just as Free Trade is ending in a tangle of vested financial interests, so democracy is ending in a tangle of words and phrases.

Thus Liberal economics have become not so much an instrument for improving the material well being of the people as a codification of so called "laws" which seek to interpret the workings of the barbarous Free Trade system. Similarly, Liberal policy has become not so much an instrument for giving effect to the will of the people as a means of preserving the crude political machinery introduced by the Reform Act of 1832. And so Liberalism, by its excessive regard for formulae, has become virtually static: the citadel of reaction. In the absence of leadership and any positive form of national spirit, the reformist urge which exists in every community has resolved itself into an endless and fruitless search for formulae. We have been groping around in the dark, looking for the particular string of words which would "cure unemployment", ensure "peace and disarmament", "restore sound finance" or "revive international trade". We have been trying to enact the letter of the law while the spirit has been altogether lacking.

This state of affairs is not altogether unconnected with the advance and popularisation of science and engineering, both of which employ formulae to a considerable extent. But the analogy is a false one. Science can obtain exactitudes which are altogether lacking in politics and economics; moreover, your true scientist regards formulae simply as stepping stones in the advance of knowledge, and is always prepared to revise or discard them as knowledge increases. The engineer again can, and must, use precision in the creation and control of machinery; but a precise mechanistic view of the affairs of men and nations is neither workable nor tolerable. It is not until we perceive each nation as a living and ever growing organism that we begin to appreciate the significance of all that is going on around us. It is the curse of the modern pseudo-democrat that he lives and thinks entirely in the abstract. Despite his solicitude for the working classes he himself rarely performs the manual labour which by keeping him in contact with real things would help to maintain his sense of values. He mistakes sentiment for sense, phrases for ideals, formulae for principles. Worse still, he is forever striving to turn the world upside down in order to make it conform with his abstractions. He would jeopardize the security of Europe in defence of "collective security"; he would have us fight in the name of peace, surrender our independence in the name of Liberty, and in general sacrifice everything for the sake of a Democracy which has ceased to have real value. Formulae. phrases, slogans. Words, words, and yet more words.

THE ILLUSION OF INTERNATIONALISM

If you set fifty men to march independently across a field, they will not all arrive at the same moment, but the probability is that all will arrive. But if you make them march together by tying them ankle to ankle, wrist to wrist, the chances are that the only ones to arrive will be those who cut themselves loose from the struggling mass.

For twenty years successive British governments have been chasing the will-o'-the-wisp of "international agreement", to the great detriment of domestic matters. At the outset of this period, there was at least this excuse, that an international war had necessitated some kind of international settlement. But as the years have gone by and conference has followed conference, settlement seems further removed than ever. Democracy has failed even more abjectly in world politics than in domestic politics, and for the same reason; namely that problems are not solved simply by throwing them open to general discussion.

These twenty years reveal themselves as a protracted attempt to achieve agreed formulae under conditions which made agreement impossible and would have made the formulae unworkable even if they had been achieved. Peace terms, self-determination, war reparations, war debts, disarmament, peace, the economics of slump and overproduction; is there a single instance in which an agreed and workable formula was discovered? On the contrary, the whole process has time and again degenerated into an elaborate farce, for example, formulae for assessing what Germany should pay, formulae for assessing how much she could pay, formulae for postponing payment, formulae for lending her money to pay with, formulae for scaling down payment, and so on.

So the international conference, from being a solution of world problems has become an excuse for the postponement of decisions, and the furtherance of intrigue. The classic example, of course, is that conference of conferences, the League of Nations, which was so overcharged with formulae that it has crumbled beneath their weight, and so rigidly associated with the status quo that it has already become an anachronism. The League Palace at Geneva should become a Museum of International Formula. The hardly less impressive, and hardly less futile, International Economic Conference would appear to have anticipated its destiny by meeting in a museum.

This breakdown clearly forces us to ask some pertinent questions. In the first place, why has international democracy failed? The answer surely is that democracy means simply majority rule, and its efficacy depends primarily upon the majority (or those who claim to represent the majority) being able to inflict their will upon the minority. Internationally, this can be done only by war or the threat of war, and a, war-weary world has so far preferred peace to League supremacy as Mussolini realised when he called the sanctions bluff in 1935.

A further answer is that the League began, and has continued, as a syndicate of the victors of the Great War, and no amount of platitudinous speech making will alter that fact in the eyes of those outside the syndicate. Had the U.S. been willing to complete the task she began in 1917, had Britain been less preoccupied with boom finance, had France concentrated a little more on peace and a little less on revenge, had courageous leadership been forthcoming at the psychological moment, the League might have been successful in abolishing that ominous formula, the "balance of power"; instead it has revived it in a new and more deadly form. But the great opportunity was thrown away; it will not soon recur.

The second question is this. Is internationalism the only approach, or even the best approach, to basic problems? Is orthodox Socialism right in insisting on its own international character? Are the Liberal economists right in insisting on international trade and finance as a pre-requisite of prosperity?

Superficially, of course, they are right; the whole world trend is towards larger political and economic units, and sooner or later an international structure of some kind will begin to take shape. But superficial thinking is one of the curses of our age, and in this case it has led to a blind disregard for elementals in favour of glib, showy, but

THE ILLUSION OF INTERNATIONALISM

fundamentally inaccurate generalisations.

Internationalism can never be a substitute for nationalism; it can only take shape as a beneficent force when it is based on sound and constructive nationalism, when its component parts are themselves healthy and vigorous. International democracy has failed, not only by reason of its own inherent weaknesses, but because it sprang from unstable national democracies. If we are to have a world League in the future, it can come about only through the voluntary association, for specific purposes, of countries which have put behind them the pettiness and irresponsibility of the democratic stage and emerged as nations fully conscious of their destiny. The mob-instinct is simply not good enough.

Thus it is that the international forces at work today, Finance, Jewry, orthodox Socialism and Communism, are far from being the expression of a spontaneous desire by the peoples of the world to achieve unity of purpose. On the contrary, they are at bottom attempts to subordinate the peoples to the dictates of a Super-State, to break down the natural claims of patriotism and racial brotherhood, and to substitute for them the rule of some soulless materialistic deity. Incredible as it may sound, community of objects brings these four forces into close, and even friendly, contact. The Communist Revolution in Russia was largely engineered by Jews and financed from Wall Street. International Socialism is largely staffed by Jews and does not hesitate to avail itself of the services of International Finance, also strongly Jewish in direction. Thus the enthusiasm of Left Wing organisations for financial sanctions, against Italy was quite in keeping with their general policy, so was their support for the economic boycott of National Socialist Germany on behalf of the Jews.

Nationalism may or may not be "narrow", but it is the only basis on which reformist energy can effectively be concentrated for many years to come, because the nation is the natural unit of human endeavour. So long as we subscribe to the theory and practice of international trade we continue at the mercy of Finance; so long as we subscribe to international pacts and treaties, any progress we may make is jeopardized by war and rumours of war. Within national frontiers we can at last get to grips with money-power; we can achieve peace and unity. Outside them we are exposed to forces we cannot control.

Nationalism need not rule out goodwill between nations; on the contrary, with the slackening of economic and military ties, social and cultural relations may well be improved. No one is the better friends with a neighbour for owing him money or entering into a legal contract with him. Goodwill and friendship are the products, not of covenants and formulae, but of mutual respect and sympathy.

THE RATIONALISATION RACKET

It has become fashionable to represent Liberty, or to be more accurate Liberalism, as a traditional British concept assaulted frontally by totalitarian doctrines. As a matter of fact, Liberalism, especially on its economic side, has been steadily undermined for many years past by those entrusted with its defence, and is now a thing of form rather than substance.

Economic Liberty or Free Trade being quite unworkable as a complete theory, some system of economic authority had to be evolved, and this authority, as we have seen, has become concentrated in. the Money system. We are, to all intents, ruled by a financial oligarchy, and this oligarchy has had no scruple in modifying the principles of Free Trade wherever they seem to impede its interests. In the name of rationalisation it has eliminated competition over a wide area by the process of merger and the institution of unified control.

But there has been a parallel attack from quite another quarter. Socialism has, from the very outset, adopted a collectivist approach to economic problems. However much it may profess to believe in political competition (i.e., the party system) it has always denounced economic competition as a prime source of insecurity, injustice and hardship to the wage-earning class. "The socialisation of the means of production, distribution and exchange" is in fact collectivism pure and simple, and as such means the end of the individual as an economic factor.

Thus we have rationalisation practiced by Finance as a means of controlling the economic system in the interests of Money and collectivism preached by Socialists as a means of controlling the economic system in the interests of Society. Motives and methods may differ somewhat in detail, but the results from the viewpoint of the individual, are nearly identical. In either case his economic status is steadily weakened until he becomes the servant of the machine.

The great danger seems to lay, not in any essential immorality of centralisation, but in its increasing employment as a panacea, a formulae, which must invariably be applied whenever the economic machine gets out of order. Admittedly the unregulated competition and unplanned enterprise of Free Trade has bequeathed us a very awkward legacy in the shape of obsolete and redundant equipment excessive multiplication of entrepreneurs and a great deal of waste and overlapping. Some measure of rationalisation or reorganisation is necessary to bring order out of chaos.

But because the task has been left to Finance, which as the mortgagee of industry has become economic dictator, the effect of rationalisation has been to create huge Money-controlled monopolies at the expense of the small entrepreneur, the small investor and the worker.

Consider a typical instance, say an industry divided, prior to rationalisation, between ten firms. Thanks to excessive competition and price-cutting among themselves, and probably foreign competition and price-cutting also, each of these firms will be heavily in debt, not only to its individual shareholders, but also, through the banks, to the financial machine. To improve the situation, protection against imports is needed, but owing to pressure on the government both from financial and Socialistic interests, this protection is not forthcoming unless the industry agrees to "reorganize". This means the elimination of individual firms as "redundant", the closing of smaller factories, and the concentration of control in the hands of a combine. This combine will obviously be the creation of those who supply the new capital required for paying compensation and re-equipping the industry with large-scale machinery; in other words, the industry becomes the subsidiary of Finance.

The superficial advantages of this process will, of course, be given considerable publicity. For instance, great stress will be laid on economies achieved in production, resulting in lower prices. The industry will be said to be more "efficient.". But analysis will reveal the fact. that these economies have been effected at the expense of labour costs. Financial costs, by reason of the outlay involved in reorganisation and mechanisation, will actually have increased. More of the

THE RATIONALISATION RACKET

selling price will be swallowed up in interest, sinking fund, reserves and depreciation, and less will be distributed as wages and salaries. So that although the rationalised industry may be providing the community with cheaper goods, it will be generating less purchasing-power, and thus rendering the community less able to purchase those goods.

This is true even if mass-production enables large masses of goods to be sold at low prices, for cheapness depends, not only upon prices, but upon the power of the community to buy. Indeed there seems very little reason to doubt that the consumption of the great volume of mass-produced goods now going into distribution is being financed to a considerable extent by the creation of fresh debts, through the hire-purchase system, through wages paid out on capital construction financed by debt, and through the losses (i.e., debts) made by industries or individuals unable to participate in rationalisation and mass-production. Even Finance itself is in process of becoming rationalized.

For many years the small investor in industrial securities, apprehensive of the hazards of his position, has been engaged in transferring his funds to the shelter of big financial institutions, such as the insurance companies and, more recently, the investment trusts. In this way the financial monopoly has not only strengthened its position, but gained, so to speak, a. human shield.

Thus the formulae, which one hears recommended on every side, rationalisation, mechanisation, and large-scale organisation, are fraught with immensely serious consequences for the community. The investing classes may uphold them as enhancing the value and earning-power of capital; Socialists may approve them as paving the way for socialisation. But the condition to which they are leading is the very negation, not only of the Liberty to which democracy pays lip-service, but of security, independence and human dignity.

SHORT-CUTS TO PARADISE

No one acquainted with popular journalism can fail to be struck with the immense number and variety of "patent remedies" offered to the public. So vast an expenditure of money and ingenuity indicates that there is a correspondingly vast market for such "remedies", which in turn suggests that a large proportion of the population is chronically or periodically disordered as a result of modern living conditions, and is for ever seeking palliatives. For be it noted that these remedies rarely attempt to deal with fundamentals, such as diet, hygiene or physical exercise; they simply profess to make life tolerable under existing conditions. Of just such a type are the various formulae brought forward as palliatives of the economic disorders from which we are now suffering, and which periodically produce spasms of acute hardship and distress, as in 1921 and 1931. And these formulae, like the "remedies" referred, to above, profess to alleviate effects without 'altering basic causes.'

Of recent years, these reformers, very naturally, have tended to concentrate on the Money-system, and let it be at once admitted that in drawing attention to the abuses of the system and the evils which flow from these abuses, they have done much good work. If they have not led people to think on the right lines, they have at least got them to think; and in these days of sloganised, mass-produced, pre-digested ideas, that in itself is something of an achievement. '

But these reformers will never go deep enough; their mechanistic prescriptions leave untouched the great spiritual and moral issues involved. You cannot alter the Money-system without altering the whole political, economic and social fabric which has been built up round it, and which is jealously guarded by its beneficiaries. Monetary reform alone, vital though it is, cannot possibly stand by itself, nor can it arouse sufficient popular support to overcome the forces of reaction.

The idea, too, that the new monetary formulae will be accepted and worked by those who administer the existing formulae and enjoy monopoly privileges will not stand examination. The very fact that the financial system cannot be criticized, either in our "free" Press or in our "popularly-elected" Parliament, bears witness to the immense and far-reaching power of Finance. This power is now by far the strongest force in the country, or for that matter in any of the democratic countries. It will not have a new system thrust upon it, and even if it could be made to accept such a system, it would soon find a way of prostituting the new formulae to it own ends. It will accept only the dictates of a power stronger than itself; that is to say the authoritarian State.

The monetary reform movement which has gone furthest in securing popular support, because no doubt it attacks on a wider front than most of the others, is Social Credit. Now the theory of Social Credit appears to rest on three main assumptions :—

(i) That the problem of production has been solved, and that if the problem of distribution can also be solved there will be progressively less work to be done (the Leisure State).

(ii) That under the existing system the processes of production do not and cannot generate sufficient purchasing power to ensure the full consumption of the product. Hence the phenomenon of "poverty in the midst of plenty".

(iii) That this undistributed portion of production costs (i.e. the difference between total costs and the sum made available as wages, salaries and profits for purchasing) represents the dividend on the national inheritance of skill and equipment, and as such should be distributed equally.

It is clear that Social Credit, like most other monetary reform proposals, rests on a single aspect of the financial system, namely its inability to circulate an adequacy of purchasing power. Its outstanding feature and the reason no doubt, for its popular appeal, are its plan for the free issue of money to make good this deficiency, and its implication that a sufficiency of real wealth already exists if only it can be distributed. It thus further impairs that sense of individual responsibility which has already been dangerously undermined, and further propagates the illusion that production can now be entrusted to the machine. Its formulae, in fact, are not so much a means whereby the social status of the individual may be raised, and his material welfare improved, as devices for getting rid of the boundless wealth which the machine is to pour into our laps.

In their main contention, Social Creditors are obviously right, monopolist Finance does keep the community chronically short of "spending money", indeed, it cannot do otherwise if it is to maintain the value of its interest-bearing debt. But this is not to say that a mere increase in the amount of money will set matters right, indeed certain parts of the financial system are already suffering from excess of money, and any further increase would dangerously inflate capital values. Any new money must be pumped in at the point where it is needed, i.e., at the bottom of the economic structure where millions of people cohabit with poverty and privation, and its distribution must be carefully supervised.

Then again, Social Creditors are on dangerous ground in assuming that if distribution is attended to, production will look after itself. There is not merely a shortage of purchasing-power; there is also a shortage of real wealth, masked by the inability of people to consume. A substantial increase in purchasing-power in advance of any corresponding increase in production can have only one effect, namely inflation of prices, wiping out any gain in consumer income and leading to undesirable speculative activity.

On these two counts alone, it is clear that the mere applications of formula will not achieve the desired end. At every point the need for authority, for driving force, and for drastic regulation of financial excess is apparent. And when Social Creditors propose to gain their ends through the agency of a Parliament which is not even allowed to discuss monetary affairs, and in the face of the strongest international force in existence, we do not need to go to Alberta to discover how far their good intentions are translatable into action.

MARXISM AND THE CLASS WAR

It is an interesting sidelight on the political apathy created by the commercialism of the Liberal era that the only major prophet of revolt during nearly a century of its existence should be a German Jew. There were, of course, notable thinkers in XIXth century Britain, but they seem to have concerned themselves mainly with the academic aspects of politics. The only 19th century movement of importance to make a positive break with the negations of Liberalism derived, and still derives, from the doctrines of Karl Marx.

As a diagnostician Marx undoubtedly showed genius. He saw clearly enough behind the smoke-screen of political liberty the growth of that economic dictatorship which had already deprived the Liberal revolution of most of its value to the people. His classification of the modern community as controllers and servants of the economic machine as exploiters and exploited, was not only justified by the horrors perpetrated in the name of Free Trade: it was the only realistic interpretation of the economics of his period.

But as a guide and philosopher, Marx is responsible for a creed of sterile hatred and internecine strife, a creed which accurately reflects the warped outlook of an embittered exile. In his insistence on a purely materialist approach to issues which are essentially moral, Marx dedicated the reformist inspiration of the late 19th and early 20th centuries to the destructive and unnatural policy of class-warfare, to the atheistic ideal of the Super-State.

Thus Socialism, which should have been the positive expression of a reawakened social conscience, and did in fact become the rallying-point of humanitarian feeling, tied itself down to the capitalist machine, the tyrannies and injustices of which it rightly condemned. For Marxism seeks, not to replace the machine with some better instrument, but to wrest it from the capitalist, and having done so to turn it upside down. This process must inevitably result in the great mass of people again falling to the bottom, leaving at the top a new set of economic dictators. Marxist Socialism, in fact, while it appeals to idealism for support, in itself singularly barren of ideals. Rather it has substituted for ideals a series of empty formula, such as "the brotherhood of man", and "international solidarity" and "dictatorship of the proletariat".

For not the least of the sterile bogs into' which Marxist doctrine has led the Left Wing movement is internationalism. Here again Socialism has been misled into fighting on its opponents' choice of battlefields and accepting the conventions of the very system which it seeks to destroy. Because Liberal capitalism is essentially international in its exploitive methods, Socialism has likewise adopted internationalism as the basis of revolution, and has thereby rendered its victory almost impossible.

Marxist Socialism, through its insistence on economic rather than racial classification, has committed itself to external Free Trade, while rejecting as a matter of course internal Free Trade. This inconsistency enormously handicaps its task of economic reform, for it is clearly impossible to raise and maintain the living-standards of workers whose products are subjected to foreign competition. The formula that living-standards must be raised in all countries through international action may be good academic logic, but has little practical validity: its effect is to gear down all real progress in Socialism to the pace set by the most backward country.

Marxism has indeed made Socialism a thing of formulae, formula derived to a large extent from the very system which it seeks to overthrow. Thus its wage-earning proletarian sheep include professors and officials with safe jobs and four-figure incomes, while its profit-earning capitalist goats include small-holders and little shopkeepers eking out a bare existence on the margin between income and outgoings. And instead of seeking to raise the status of the proletariat it aims at reducing the whole community to their level.

The goal of Socialism is itself a triumph of formulae making. "The socialisation of the means of production, distribution and exchange, the whole to be controlled by a democratically organised state in the interests of the entire community" will not stand detailed analysis. For democratic organisations, as experience has shown, certainly do not represent the entire community; nor are they in any way adapted for the immense responsibilities which complete socialisation implies. In fact, in taking over democracy, which is full brother to Free Trade and capitalism, Socialism has greatly weakened its claim to be the creed of the future. If the State is to be the controller of a highly complex economic system, it must be a State built up on something a good deal sounder than the mass-vote.

It is the tragedy of International Socialism that it has never got beyond Karl Marx. It has watched the doctrine of class-warfare degenerate into obsolete formulae; it has seen other problems, more urgent and more vital arise, it has seen a new spirit stirring in every civilized nation. And it has taken root as a vested interest, Marxism Ltd., while its opportunities have gone riding by. It may have retained its respectability; it may have become the second political party; it may have furnished honorable careers for its more astute members; but it is no longer the movement of revolt; it no longer leads the fight against Money and the Machine.

Nor is there any indication that the world as a whole is moving Marx-ward. Socialism has a remarkable record of failure and incompetence. Only in Scandinavia, where its tenets seem to be tempered with sturdy Nordic common sense, has it shown any signs of permanence. One does not expect the Socialist Revolution to be accomplished overnight and without a certain amount of disorder and even bloodshed. But nowhere has the Socialist State begun to take shape out of the confusion.

"The Russian" Revolution was captured without much difficulty by the businesslike Bolsheviks; in Spain much the same would have happened if the national spirit had not risen in disgust. In Italy and Germany, International Socialism crumbled before the rapid advance of National Socialism. In Britain, MacDonald, the Scottish demagogue, fell ignominiously into the arms of his opponents; in France, Blum, the Jewish millionaire, has wobbled ingloriously between

Finance and the Red Flag. The soul of Socialism has been atrophied by formulae; its faith has become neurotic hysteria; with the rest of the democratic paraphernalia it is passing into the discard of history.

ON TO COMMUNISM

There is no particular mystery about the theory of Communism, for it is the logical conclusion of Marxist Socialism. If one accepts the proposition that private ownership and abuse of capital is the source of all evil then it is but a step to the corollary that private ownership of any property is immoral. For property, argues the Communist, is the product of capitalist exploitation, and as such has been unfairly appropriated from the common stock. Abolish private property, and the incentive for exploitation disappears.

Thus there is little difficulty in investing Communism with a fine aurora of moral, and even religious, sanctity, or in rendering it attractive to certain types of intellect. The academic mind, in particular, because it is more accustomed to weighing, formula than to dealing with realities, and perhaps, too, because it sets little store by property, is readily disposed to view the property-less society as a not altogether undesirable possibility. And it is not lost upon it that in Communist Russia the "intelligentsia" share with the bureaucracy the privileges of aristocracy.

But in practice Communism is materialistic, vengeful and ruthless. It perceives, though it will not always admit, that love of property is deeply ingrained in human nature, and that nothing short of an earthquake will separate the ordinary citizen from his habit of accumulation. It perceives too that so long as men have the status and dignity which possessions give them, they will resist to the uttermost the State absolutism which is indispensable to Communist society. Therefore it must first stage the earthquake; and since the Communist believes firmly that the end justifies the means, he has become earthquake-maker to the world at large, a professional incendiary, the remorseless agent of destruction.

In Russia the task was not too difficult, for there has always existed in that country. a huge mass of property-less persons inured to a ruthless State absolutism. Lenin and Trotsky, experienced revolutionaries with no scruples, found the tepid Liberal-Socialist revolution of Kerensky stuck on a dead centre. They galvanised it into a burst of intense activity which made them masters of Russia before the great mass of her population were aware of it. Even so, it cost upwards of eight million lives, and an incalculable amount of misery and suffering, before the Soviet regime was established. And now that the Soviet has, so to speak, come of age, we discover that while the State absolutism is there in all conscience, the society which it has produced seems to have much more in common with medieval despotism than with the theory of Communism. At any rate it hardly seems the kind of culture which smug Western democrats can safely welcome to their bourgeois bosoms.

Thus, while Communist theory has attracted the abstractionist intellectual, Communist practice has attracted quite another type of mind, namely the man with a grudge, not merely against a class or a system, but against society, the man who feels that he has nothing to lose and something to gain by a general upheaval. Sometimes he is an honest worker embittered by injustice or misfortune sometimes he is a fanatical Socialist grown weary of, the "gradualness" of his party. But, as often as not he is one of the world's misfits, without ties, without hope, often without nationality, a denizen of the jungle which exists somewhere in every big city. For the Moscow agent knows his job, he does not waste time or money on those who have something to preserve, but recruits his shock-troops for the assault on civilization from the ranks of those to whom civilization means nothing but loot withheld.

So Communism is essentially destructive. Its ideal (or perhaps more accurately its mirage) may be that of a purified society, but the process of purification involves the destruction of all that has gone before, good, bad and indifferent, race, religion, culture, class, property. Nor does the process end when its own materialistic philosophy is established, for it must be continually purging itself of all who show any signs of reversion to a more natural way of life.

THE BUREAUCRATIC STATE

Thus the condition with which we are now threatened, if the immediate calamity of war does not intervene, is the diametric backswing from Liberalism. Whether we continue, in the name of Democracy, to permit the further encroachments of Finance until everything is one huge Money controlled monopoly, or whether we drift, through the Social-Democrat phase, into Communism, there is clearly an end to the individual man on which Liberalism was built. We shall be exhorted to defend to the last ditch that bedraggled symbol of democracy, the mass-vote, only to find that it has lost all power to preserve to us the realities of life, personal freedom, security, justice, property, religion and patriotism.

It was the tragic blunder of Liberalism that it believed that a collection of free individuals would automatically produce economic justice and good government. Out of the confusion thus created emerged the octopus of International Finance and its step-sister International Communism, neither of which rates the individual higher than a pawn in its arrangement of world affairs. If we do not wish to say farewell to the spiritual things of life, to patriotism, to religion, to independence and enterprise, we must arouse the spirit of our nation to give battle to the forces of materialism.

If it was Liberalism which liberated the evil genii of Finance, it is Socialism which has shirked the responsibility of putting it back in its bottle, for Socialism has so far failed to perceive that the real struggle is not between class and class for the control of the machine, but between Man and the machine itself. Its painstaking internationalism, its childish devotion to the doctrines of Marx, have blinded it to the great issue of modem times, which is whether Man organised on natural racial and national lines can recapture control of this ruthless juggernaut, Money-plus-Machine-Power, or whether he will sink into ignoble insignificance as its slave.

The Socialist remedy, in fact, is strangely akin to the disease, for, as we have seen, there is little to choose between the effects of financial monopoly and the effects of socialisation. The combine will, presumably, be replaced by a government department; the financier will, presumably, be replaced by a bureaucrat; but otherwise the process of monopolisation will go on much as before, though possibly at a faster pace for having the authority of the State behind it. There is no suggestion of any restoration to the individual of the functions and rights which have been filched from him.

Thus the senior reformist organisation is put in the anomalous position of having its work done for it by its nominal opponents. "Private ownership is wasteful and inefficient," says the Socialist. "Quite so," says Finance, "see how we are replacing it with our big combines, which are really public undertakings in disguise." "Capitalism sweats the worker," says the Socialist. "Quite so," says Finance, "see what wonderful amenities we are providing for him, what luxurious cinemas, what generous competitions, what sensational newspapers."

"Capitalism denies the masses the fruits of their toil," says the Socialist. "Quite so," says Finance, "see what an abundance of cheap goods are provided by mass-production and hire-purchase. See what an abundance of cheap food our international tribute system brings to these shores. My dear fellow, we are obviously aiming at the same goal."

And so long as we employ purely materialist standards, there would appear to be little that socialisation can do that is not already being done by Finance. The bureaucrat, certainly, will probably be rather less ruthless and less efficient than the financier, because he is not paid by results. For which reason nothing is more likely than that the Socialist State will come to terms with Finance.

After all, your financial magnate ceases after a certain point, to accumulate money for money's sake. His objective becomes, not money, but the power which money gives, and as a State official this power would be regularised and confirmed. There are ominous signs already to be observed in the State-appointed Commissions which are springing up all over the industrial map, particularly, in the sphere of agriculture. The Commissioners (dare one say Kommissars?) are for the most part drawn from the ranks of Big Business or the bureaucracy; rarely are they representative of the industry which they are appointed to regulate. And we are still a "democratic country" !

This, then, is the paradise to which Socialists would steer us, supposing they are able to escape the Scylla of International Finance and the Charybdis of International Communism. A paradise staffed and managed exclusively by bureaucrats, carefully graded, immaculately conscientious, rising tier by tier, Board by Board, Department by Department, to the supreme deity of the Socialised State. Can we believe that this massive edifice will really be controlled by "democratic organisations", that the ribald tongues of M.P. s will really be allowed to criticise its wonderful workings? Will not the socialised machine be as sacred and inviolate as the financial machine?

No wonder the Labour party is the spiritual home of the great and growing class of salaried public servants, who look to exploit the Socialist Revolution just as enthusiastically and as thoroughly as the bourgeoisie exploited the Liberal Revolution. It is a dear, good, conscientious class, honestly convinced that the "workers" who are to stage the revolution will be quite unable to use it except by direction of the bureaucracy; and equally convinced that all problems, will be settled as soon as everyone has an official position and salary.

The bureaucratic state. What a vista to set before Britain, the leader in world-adventure, the mistress of a quarter of the globe — the vista of some drab corridor in a public institution. If democracy is a vision of an endless succession of chairmen making endless, fatuous, fact-dodging speeches, then Socialism is a vision of an endless series of Government officials tucking away in neat pigeon-holes the hopes and ambitions of the British people.

PART III - REBIRTH

THE DISINTEGRATION OF SOCIALISM

So far we have been applying the term "Socialist" to the school of thought which derives directly from Karl Marx and which makes "socialisation" (i.e., State monopoly) its goal. This is primarily a matter of convenience, the Marxist internationalist school being the senior group, and therefore most readily identified in the public mind with Socialism.

But Socialism is really a generic rather than a specific term. Anyone who' views society primarily as a collection of individuals and gives priority to the liberty of the individual is a Liberal, no matter how sympathetic he may feel towards schemes of social amelioration. Conversely, anyone who feels that the individual can exist and find expression only as a member of an organised society (national or international) is a Socialist, no matter how much he may talk about liberty and democracy. And the fact that there are quite a number of people desirous of making the best of both worlds, as for instance by retaining their own liberty of thought and action while making use of all that an organised society has to offer, does not really affect the distinction. Socialism as a creed is not necessarily discredited by careerist exponents.

Socialism is thus seen to be a sort of blanket term covering the greater part of modern outlook. Its right wing shades imperceptibly into the emasculated Liberalism of the Social-Democrats; its left wing stretches beyond the pale of Western ethics and Christian values into Communism. Its tenets run the whole gamut from the mild humanitarianism of Lansbury. to the ruthless materialism of Stalin.

Socialism as a coherent political force is thus ceasing to exist. In its efforts to mobilise every revolt against debased Liberalism, every urge towards a more intelligent scheme of life, every reawakening of the social conscience, it has so enlarged its borders that it has lost purpose and direction. Its more conservative elements are for ever seeking a compromise with Liberal capitalism, a search which has given rise to bureaucratic monstrosities like the L.P.T.B., the Central Electricity Commission and the Agricultural Marketing Boards. Its more advanced and intransigent elements are moving steadily up the Marxian path towards Communism, naturally with the active assistance and encouragement of Moscow.

Nowhere has the Socialist State been more than a transitional stage; and as the years go by the prospects of such a State grow steadily more dim. Probably the nearest which we shall get to it is the queer and unlovely mixture of bureaucracy and financial monopoly which now seems to be the accepted formula for making good the ravages of Free Trade. The big capitalist obviously has a use for Socialism in that it regularises and confirms his domination over his smaller brethren; he has no objection to State-monopoly so long as he is the medium through which the State works. Conversely, the theoretical Socialist has no objection to rationalisation and trustification so long as he can deck it out in the garments of public ownership.

But this bastard offspring of Finance and Socialism, this consummation of materialism, has one great defect which rules it out for ever in the eyes of all men of spirit. It has no life: it does not and cannot live. It has no soul above its own statistics. For a year or two it may offer a soulless security to the proletariat; it may even offer the bedeviled small capitalist a way of escape into proletarianism. It may offer leisure, a release from the machine in order to provide opportunity for machine-made culture. But it has no soul, and because it has no soul, it will perish.

Equally the Western mind will revolt against the materialist philosophy of the slave-State of Communism. For a time, the intellectual may toy with the theory in a rare atmosphere of detachment; for a time the outcast may sweeten his misery with dreams of organised loot amid the wreckage of society. But the example of Russia has not been lost upon the West, despite the cloud of propaganda and counter-propaganda in which it has been enveloped. The growing resentment of official Labour at the incursions of Communist agents, though not perhaps entirely disinterested, is symbolical of the attitude of Britain. We will not, under any consideration, take orders from a foreign source. The rock on which Communism will batter itself to pieces is the rock on which true statesmanship must build - the rock of national consciousness.

This conclusion is no mere flourish of dialectic: it is the great lesson of modern European history. In one country after another, the forces of Marxism have gained the ascendant only to crumble and disintegrate in the face of resurgent nationalism. For love of country, pride of race, and community of tradition can give birth to great disciplined mass-movements, where "Popular Fronts" breed only the intensive strife of rival factions. Communism fails because there is no community of spirit.

There is one point, and one point only, at which Socialism can crystallise into a coherent, vital entity, and galvanise its bewildered followers into a definite course of action; and that is the point at which the national leader emerges, with a clear-cut programme and an unambiguous appeal to national spirit. Here at once are two unmistakable points of difference between Fascism and the Socialistic confusion from which it springs, leadership and nationalism, as opposed to committeeism and internationalism.

Herein are the secrets of the amazing success of the Fascist Revolution, which in two decades has accomplished more than has been achieved by a century of Marxist Socialism. It is unquestionably a popular movement, but it has given expression to popular feeling, not by cherishing all the old formulae and vested interests of democracy, but by discarding them wholesale. It is an idealistic movement, but it has built up its ideals on the natural foundations of race and soil. "It may have hitched its wagon to a star, but at least it has kept its wheels on the ground."[3] Above all, it has given the people something vastly more satisfying than words and phrases, the formulae of reform; it has given them action, movement, much of it symbolism and pageantry, no doubt, but behind it the reality of concrete achievement.

---
3 A.J.Penty

THE RE-EMERGENCE OF LEADERSHIP

It is fashionable among the pseudo-democrats to label Fascism "dictatorship". The object, of course, is to sustain the illusion that the party politics of democracy represent popular government, while Fascism is an imposed autocracy. But in point, of fact, the epithet is useful in that it directs attention to the keystone of Fascist organisation, leadership.

There is nothing intrinsically antipathetic or incongruous, in personal leadership and popular government. On the contrary, a leader holding office on the strength of his personal appeal to the electorate is very much more likely to give effect to the wishes of that electorate than any party caucus. And it is, as we have seen, the tragedy of Socialism, as of democracy, that it has discarded ideals, for formulae, leadership for committeeism.

Over and over again in democratic history has a prospective leader arisen, only to be dragged back into the nick of party politics by that factionalism which is inherent in democracy and, in fact, one of the chief virtues claimed for it. If we seek a modern example we need go no further back than David Lloyd George. Gaining office in the first place as an uncompromising party politician, it was not until the crisis of the Great War had temporarily submerged sectional interests and set a premium on directness of thought and action, that he acquired true breadth and depth of statesmanship.

Whatever may be said of his conduct of military policy in those dark days, there can be no doubt whatever that the forceful personality and unquenchable vitality of this fiery little Welshman were one of the deciding factors in the struggle. People believed in him, not because they liked him or his political associations, but because he stood before them as a leader of decision, imagination and courage; and because they believed, they were enabled to endure. He fell in the end because factional interests, once released from "the ties of common funk," would no longer tolerate their subordination to national interests.

SPRING COMES AGAIN

Consider, by way of comparison, the so-called leaders of post-War British politics; Stanley Baldwin, consummate strategist and accomplished actor, yet first and always a party man, striving to make Britain safe for his class; Ramsay MacDonald, gifted orator with an uncanny knack of handling men, almost sublime in the intense egotism which made him renounce his country in 1916 and his political creed in 1931; Winston Churchill, the supreme adventurer, so patently eager to make personal capital of the emotions of the moment that even the parties have learnt to mistrust him; Neville Chamberlain, the plodder, honest, within the limits of his prim Victorianism, but utterly incapable of escaping from his financial associations. Atlee, Dalton and Cripps, soft-handed exploiters of the workers' vote, convinced only of one thing, that the world must end with the eclipse of the party politician.

It seems almost farcical to set these petty strategists these wordy careerists beside the leaders of the new revolution. Consider Benito Mussolini, the blacksmith's son, uncompromising Socialist until bitter travail taught him that Socialism must be reborn; ascetic, visionary, yet a brilliant empiricist, creating as he went new methods, new values, a new Italy, Rome reborn, yet ever and always one of the people. Consider Adolf Hitler, the son of Austrian peasants, romantic to the point of mysticism, clinging desperately to his immense ideals in the face of bitter defeat, identifying himself more and more with the spirit of the German race till he could give at last triumphant expression to that spirit. Consider Franco, brilliant soldier and constructive thinker, born an aristocrat, yet refusing to take the easy path back into traditionalism, holding fast amid bloody internecine strife to the vision of a new and united Spain. And Oswald Mosley, the very embodiment of English tradition, an aristocrat proving his claim to aristocracy by personal leadership, by sacrificing career class, party and wealth to his uncompromising championship of the British people.

Superficially, these, four men have little in common. Mussolini was a school-teacher turned journalist, Hitler a painter, Franco and Mosley professional soldiers. Conventionally speaking, the first two are democrats, the second two aristocrats. Yet there is about each of

THE RE-EMERGENCE OF LEADERSHIP

them that which stamps them as men of destiny, a white-hot intensity of purpose, a simplicity of mind which consecrates everything to the great task, an immense belief in the integrity of Western civilization as a whole and the destiny of their own countries in particular.

Fundamentally they are fighters, not fighters against their fellow-men, for each has passed through the fiery crucible of war and knows to the last agonising detail what war is: but fighters against the shams and hypocrisies; the bland deceits; the futilities, of their age; scorning its facile formulae and rousing the West to battle with those twin Molochs; Finance and Communism.

Between these men and the dope-peddling, phrase-making crew which now bestrides the decrepit carcass of democracy, there can be nothing in common. To the pseudo-democrat there can be nothing more distasteful than a return to the primitive form of democracy, the programme of popular action, the direct appeal to the people. To the Fascist leader there can be nothing more distasteful than the clutter of parties, groups, caucuses and vested interests which has sprung up between government and the governed. Therein lies the origin of the unveiled hatred of the pseudo-democrat for the leader, the unveiled contempt of the leader for democracy as practiced today.

For it must be clearly understood that Fascist leadership of today is no mere revival of the military dictatorships of the past. The strength of Mussolini lies not only in the fact that he has avenged the defeat of Adowa and restored the African Empire, rebuilt Rome and drained the Pontine Marshes, but in the still more impressive fact that he is Italy, the very embodiment of the new spirit which has made these things possible. Even so, Hitler is much more than the man who broke the degradation of Versailles and built the Greater Reich: he is the new Germany, the land of hope resurgent. And when thousands cheer Mosley in the East End of London, it is not only because he is a great Englishman with a unique gift for expressing English ideals in plain language, but because he can and does identify himself with that spirit of true patriotism which still lingers in every English heart.

The question then arises. If personal leadership is the keystone of the Fascist arch, is it not also its weakest spot, for even men who live like athletes are still mortal? The best answer is to be found in Fascist organisation. There are no committees in this organisation, consequently no jockeying for position, no clique-making, no "waiting for dead men's shoes" From top to bottom the principle of leadership is in force, consequently there is a steady up-growth of men and women, young for the most part, who have proved themselves fitted for responsibility, and from these future national leaders are chosen. Moreover, as office is never regarded as a reward for party service, but as a responsibility which entails great personal sacrifice, Fascism makes short work of the mere careerist.

THE SPIRIT OF FASCISM

It is often urged against Fascism that there is nothing original in its policy. Youth movements, labour service, agricultural revival have long been advocated outside its ranks; economic nationalism in some form or other is a stock policy all over the world; even the Corporate State owes much (though by no means all) to guild-Socialism. If Fascism ended with Fascist policy, the criticism would be valid.

But the very fact that these policies in the absence of Fascism are not carried out, or carried out with highly imperfect results, surely proves that policy is not all, that the reason why Fascism achieves where democracy fails is because it possesses something vital. Nor is compulsion the missing factor for coercion has been applied longer and with far more ruthlessness in Soviet Russia than in the Fascist countries, yet its achievements have been much less. No, the secret of Fascism is its semi-religious fervour, the desperate eleventh-hour struggle of Western civilisation for the recapture of its soul, the revolt of man against the tyranny of Money and the Machine..

So far as Britain is concerned, the easiest way to visualise this spirit is to recall the national unity of 1914-18, when nothing else seemed to matter but the winning of the war. Add to this spirit of unity the patient loyalty and self-sacrifice which built up the Labour movement, plus the fiery ardour of a religious revival. Then one begins to understand the spirit which enables men and women to march steadfastly through a barrage of brickbats and spittle, which enables raw lads and cultured women to mount their soapboxes night after night in the pouring rain, which enables the retired colonel cheerfully to accept the orders of a shop assistant, which enables men to risk their livelihood and give up their scanty leisure for the sake of an ideal, which enabled Mosley and a handful of devoted friends to build anew on the wreckage of the New Party.

Fascism is militant. Born everywhere in ridicule, surviving only in defiance of bitter opposition, riding out wave after wave of adversity, it could hardly be anything but a fighting creed. Distortion of this fundamental truth has produced the parrot-cry that "Fascism means war." Yet when the figures come to be analysed it will be found that the numbers slain in the name of Fascism are infinitely less than those slain in the name of Communism in its various forms. And it is a fact that most of the war-talk which has kept the world, in a state of jitters for the last two years emanates from those whose keen desire it is that the peoples of Europe should "smash Fascism" on their behalf. Hell holds no fury like a Marxist scorned.'

Fascism makes no facile appeal. It has nothing to offer its adherents save arduous service. It has no soft jobs, no patronage, none of the legalised bribery at which the democratic parties connive. . . It demands discipline and sacrifice; it gives nothing but pride of service and the satisfaction of loyal comradeship.

What, then, are its attractions in an age which has been taught to despise discipline and seek easy pleasures? Is it not that the world has come, through bitter experience, to realise the folly and sterility of the mob-mentality, the sheep-like complacency which takes no thought for the future so long as it has grass in front of it? Is it not that the harshness and injustice of the industrial system have at last aroused' the crusading spirit which hitherto could find expression only in the hate-born sterilities of Karl Marx?

Fascism is commonly said to be movement of youth. This is largely true. Young Britain has looked in the future, and found therein little inspiration; it makes hay of the old shibboleths, democracy, party loyalty, the inevitability of slumps and wars, "sound" finance, and the deference due to those who have muddled away the national heritage. But, hitherto there has been nothing set in their place. Thirty, twenty, or even ten years ago, most young men and women with a natural urge to make the world a better place, drifted into the Labour Party. Today they are attracted to Fascism, not only because its realist creed survives better the critical analysis of modern youth, but because the tide of patriotism, damned back in the nineteen-twenties by misdirected pacifism, is running strongly again.

THE SPIRIT OF FASCISM

But the movement is not exclusively one of youth. Its pioneers and its solid core have always been, in Britain as elsewhere, those who having already given something for their country have no wish to see that something frittered away. The war veteran, the retired administrator and the matron are the connecting link between youth and tradition.

For those who care to see, the Fascist spirit is something fine and unselfish, almost breath-taking in its intensity and sincerity. Therein lays perhaps the greatest danger of the future. A political creed which is itself akin to a religion can hardly avoid contact with the Churches.

This is not to say that Fascism is in any respect anti-religious, still less is it anti-Christian. Indeed it is probably true to say that Christianity is today more secure inside the Fascist countries than outside them.

The more obvious danger lies in the fact that certain of the clergy have unmistakably identified themselves with political creeds, apparently oblivious of the example of Christ himself, who, despite obvious temptations held steadfastly aloof from the politics of His day. If men occupying responsible positions as Ministers of God deliberately take part in political controversies, they are likely to be regarded as camouflaged politicians and treated accordingly.

The less obvious, but much greater danger lies in the way in which Fascism mobilises and gives expression to those spiritual qualities of service and sacrifice which should be the basis of all religion, but which, in a materialistic age, have been largely lost to the Churches. For Liberalism has encouraged the habit of keeping religion, business and politics, in separate psychological compartments, and religion has suffered thereby.

Will the Churches regard this new fount of inspiration as a challenge to their authority? Or will they welcome it as a source of religious revival? Will they allow themselves to become associated with the, forces of reaction? Or will they play their part in the renaissance of the West? That is a question which only the Churches themselves can answer.

As the atmosphere becomes more tense, as the struggle between Fascism and its opponents approaches its final stages, an immense body of sincere Christians, both inside and outside the Churches, will move in its direction, no matter what attitude the Churches take up. One of the crucial questions of the future is whether or not Christianity will spring renewed from the fresh-tilled ground, and if so, in what form.

TOLERANCE AND THE TOTALITARIAN CONCEPT

The word "tolerance" is nowadays almost as sorely overworked as "Liberty". It is open to precisely the same objections. As an ideal, strictly conditioned by other ideals, tolerance is desirable; as a basis for social organisation it fails lamentably. For any advance towards righteousness and justice inevitably entails intolerance of evil and injustice. Indeed the abolition of things like slavery and child-labour was only achieved by the victory of intolerance over tolerance.

It is significant that tolerance is most loudly preached by those who have little to tolerate. The well-fed have no difficulty in tolerating those who speculate in foodstuffs and play tricks with the poor man's budget. The West-Ender who enjoys Jewish artistry on the stage or in the concert hall waxes indignant with the "racial prejudices" of East-Enders who have to work for and amongst Jews. The comfortable rentier who regards politics as just another game, has little sympathy for those who would abolish the party system in order to mobilise national energies in the national interest.

The only people who have a right to tolerance are those who have to put up with its results; and since in the case of political and economic issues, it is the great mass of the population which has to put up with the results, tolerance on the part of those charged with the duty of government all too often covers the shirking of responsibilities.

Tolerance of political opposition, as we have seen, is .a "virtue" enforced on democracy by the fact that party politics can never provide fully representative government. This tolerance means, only too often, that an entrenched group can not only obstruct government, but inflict great hardship on the rest of the community and even endanger national security. Most of us can remember what those fine volunteer soldiers of 1914-15 endured in Flanders because a democratic government at home tolerated strike-tactics among munitions workers; what is not always realised is that those strike-tactics originated in official tolerance of rank profiteering.

SPRING COMES AGAIN

The need today is not of more tolerance, but of less, lest the ensuing reactions bring excesses of intolerance. People will not tolerate much longer the vulgar ostentation of wealth by a few while poverty and unemployment are rife, the monopolisation of the Money-system by a little group of vested interests, the subordination of urgent domestic problems to a political craze for foreign affairs. True statesmanship would perceive that intolerance employed by government as a surgeon's knife is preferable to intolerance employed by an outraged mob as a meat-axe.

The tasks confronting Britain in the next decade will call for the output of at least as much national effort as was required in the Great War. If we are to retain our nationhood and self-respect, we have not only got to avert the war and the slump which now threaten us, we have got to find our soul again, regain our economic independence, abolish poverty and set up standards of social and economic justice in keeping with our noble heritage and vast resources. Will the tolerance of selfishness, class-consciousness, obstruction and factionalism better fit us for this task?

Scientific jargon often misleads by its very abstruseness. "Totalitarianism", or worse still "totalitarianisation", is terrifying; it has, too, a foreign ring. "Team-work", on the other hand, is homely and essentially English; it expresses something with which the Briton is perfectly familiar and which he usually admires; yet it also expresses that concept of Fascism which he is taught to dread under the horrific title of "totalitarianism". Subtle are the ways of propagandists.

Team-work is implicit in the Fascist philosophy, just as it is implicit in the symbolical fasces. That it involves some measure of compulsion is admitted, but justice demands some measure of compulsion. Why should ten members of a football team be made to lose their matches because the eleventh member declines to play for his side? In any team that is a team, an offending member is either made to mend his ways or leave the team. His conduct, in fact, is considered intolerable. That is precisely the attitude of the Fascist leader or captain towards obstructive or discordant elements in the State: refugee propaganda notwithstanding.

TOLERANCE AND THE TOTALITARIAN CONCEPT

Thus the difference between democracy and Fascism is, broadly speaking, the difference between the committee and the team system. The committee system gives each member equal weight on every issue, no matter what his qualifications, and such decisions as are arrived at, usually after needless delay, are at best compromises, crude averages of divergent and often discordant views. It also provides every member with an opportunity to evade responsibility. The team system gives each member responsibility for specific jobs, but vests supreme responsibility in the captain, who is thus able to decide each issue on its merits and give full expression to the policy which he has been elected to carry out. And the fact that many committees adopt the plan of saying "yes" to the views of their more expert or more energetic members is a tacit admission 'of the principle of leadership.

The only reason for the survival of the committee system is that it has become a vested interest, a happy hunting ground for those who have a gift for office without responsibility. These persons have naturally fostered the superstition (in which they themselves no doubt firmly believe) that no right decision can possibly be arrived at unless a pro and a con are elaborately formulated and enthusiastically argued. Perhaps this is why lawyers figure so prominently in Parliament.

No discussion of tolerance would be complete without reference to the Jewish problem. Fascism is often condemned out of hand because it recognises the existence of this problem and attempts to solve it, sometimes in ways which are distasteful to the smug bourgeois mind. Indeed no small part of the anti-Fascist agitation in this country, and with it the menace of war, is directly attributable to motives of retaliation which are perhaps natural in the Jews themselves, but which are utterly inconsistent with British interests. A war of revenge on behalf of another race would be a short-cut to disaster. Considered apart, the Jew has certain admirable qualities. He is alert, intelligent, artistic in certain spheres, he is notably industrious. He maintains the family bond; he is good to his women and children, and the way in which he has remained loyal to his race and creed through centuries of exile and dispersion is one of the marvels of history.

But the Jew cannot be considered apart; he must be considered in relation to his Gentile hosts. For the existence of Jews in any numbers in a Western community is invariably a disturbing factor, and often a demoralising one. There are just two attitudes which can be adopted in regard to the Jewish issue. One can pretend that it does not exist, agreeing perhaps with Kipling that "Israel is a race to leave alone. It abets disorder". Or one can acknowledge its potentialities for mischief and seek to remove them.

The first attitude is that of the so-called democracies. If one accepts, as Liberalism does, the whole theory of "Liberty and Equality," one must refuse to perceive any distinction between Eastern Jew and Western Gentile; one must assume that the legal process of naturalisation by some mystic formula transforms an obvious exotic into a "natural" Briton, Frenchman or American; one must be blind to a growing condition of tension at points of contact, and when anti-Semitism actually breaks out, attribute it to prejudice or the machinations of evilly disposed persons.

The second attitude is that of Fascism. If one believes that nationalism is a vital factor in human progress, one can only regard as an acute problem the existence within the State of an intensely race-conscious exotic community with strong international affiliations. If one perceives that irresponsible Money-power is the greatest enemy of our day, one must profoundly mistrust the infiltration of those whose outstanding characteristic is a gift for handling money. If one realises that the impact of Eastern culture and moral standards on Western culture and moral standards must inevitably produce a clash, then one does not dismiss the phenomenon of anti-Semitism, from Poland to the U.S., from Italy to East London as an extraordinary manifestation of prejudice.

Whether or not the Jews regard it as a part of their racial destiny systematically to exploit Gentiles, the ugly fact remains that millions of Gentiles do positively identify Jews with exploitation and those who wear the shoe know best where it pinches. Whether or not the Jews play a part disproportionate to their numbers in anti-social activities, it is nevertheless true that they engage in dealing and usury rather than the production of wealth, and that their natural acquisitiveness and love of ostentation arouses the resentment of those among whom they dwell.

Anti-Semitism naturally varies in intensity according to the intensity of Jewish penetration, a fact which is of peculiar significance in this country at the present time. The existing German campaign is the natural reaction to the long period of poverty, misery, and degradation which came between the Armistice and the advent of National Socialist government, and which Jewry exploited to its own advantage. Israel indeed cannot be "left alone" unless and until it leaves the Gentile alone.

There is then but one solution to remove anti-Semitism by removing the Semite, to relieve irritation by removing the irritant, to end the circumstances which have made the Jew a parasite by bringing about the re-integration of the Jewish nation. If exile and dispersion have made the Jew a hated and often persecuted alien, then the sooner exile and dispersion end the better for mankind, and in particular the Jew.

There are still available sparsely populated but fertile areas, in Africa, in South America, in Asiatic Russia, in which a re-united Jewish race could create anew its nationality and establish a new home. In regaining contact with the soil it would set the Jewish character on a broader basis in regaining national dignity and it would triumphantly fulfil its racial destiny. In withdrawing its disturbing influence from other nations, it would obtain peace and goodwill in place of strife and animosity.

If the Fascist Revolution can bring about the re-integration of Jewry, and thus bring to an end the Jewish problem as it affects the West, it will not be the least of its achievements.

UNITY, EQUITY, SECURITY

Liberty, Equality, Fraternity, was the watchwords of the Liberal Revolution. Unity, Equity, Security are the watchwords of the Fascist Revolution. The Fascist trinity may or may not have higher ethical value than the Liberal trinity. The point is that they have higher real value to Man under the circumstances in which he finds himself today.

Unity is the first degree in Fascism, the pre-requisite of achievement. Whenever and wherever men and women band themselves together, sinking all personal prejudice and ambition, for the attainment of a common end, for the fulfillment of a common ideal, there is a fasces in being. It was Mussolini's "bundles" that made possible the March on Rome; it is Mosley's "action teams" that are making possible a Greater Britain.

But Unity is essentially a condition, and Fascism is more than a condition; it is an act. Fascist Unity is forged in action as a sprawling coat is knit together by honest work. It is not the static fellowship of a formal association but the vital comradeship of a seasoned refinement, not the "coalition" of politicians thrown together by "ties of common-funk," but the unity of a team girded for action.

And there is a need for action in Britain today, action to secure the establishment on a lasting footing of the great principle of Equity. Not Justice alone, not merely the precise formulae of the law courts, but the living principle of the Fair Deal.

Who will deny that such action is needed? We have at our disposal, actual or potential, sufficient real wealth to give to every Briton all the necessities, most of the comforts, and many of the luxuries of life. We can also give to every Briton real opportunities for culture recreation, and mental and physical development. These things will not fall into our laps at the sound of a magic formula, nor are they to be obtained simply by bumping off a few "capitalists". They mean work and organisation: more difficult still, they mean scrapping old ideas and building up new ones. But, they can be got, and got they will be, if we can generate sufficient national unity and purpose.

And yet at the present time there is not even an approach either to adequate production or to equitable distribution. A huge army of producers stands idle, while natural resources lie unused or fall into dereliction. The men who till the soil and dig the coal and weave the cloth and stoke the boilers must eat stale food, live in poky rooms, and wear the cheapest clothing, while a few superior beings live softer lives than is good for their health. Therefore, there is a great need for Equity, Equity of production which would allot to each his fair share of work, so that the common wealth might be released for common use. And Equity of distribution which would allot to each a fair share of the product.

There is nothing new in all this. Socialists and even Communists have been preaching the better distribution of work and wealth for decades past. But the Socialist because he inherited, so to speak, the rather discredited Liberal legend of equality, has somehow got Equality - and Equity inextricably confused. And since the best way (if not the only way) even to approach Equality is to deny men the opportunity to exercise inequality, he has committed himself to a concept of nationalisation or State monopoly which is by no means palatable to the majority of Britons. And so in Socialist ideology, the real principle of Equity, which consists in apportioning work according to ability, rewards according to deserts, and responsibilities according to capacity, has been obscured by the cloudy abstraction of Equality, which comes dangerously near violating several rules of nature.

Fascists have not so far made this mistake. They prefer to build upwards - from existing facts towards an attainable ideal, instead of downwards from an unattainable ideal towards existing facts. They recognise that the existing condition of inefficiency and inequity is due not so much to the individual ownership of capital (which is, after all, a perfectly natural phenomenon), as to a lack of co-operation, plus a vicious theory of economics, plus the monopolist tactics of certain groups. They believe in national team-work rather than in nationalisation, in the corporate State rather than in State monopoly.

The establishment of Equity in economic matters will, of itself lead to that kind of Security which means so much to us all, namely, security against poverty, unemployment and destitution, against exploitation, against an uncared-for old age. The price will be Liberty, the Liberty of those forces which now contribute so much to insecurity, the Stock Exchange the manipulated market, the ruthless combine the sensation mongering Press the political adventurer. And it is a price which we can well afford to pay.

And while Fascism is opposed to State monopoly in production and distribution as a system unsuited to the Western temperament, it by no means rules out the direct responsibilities of the State in specific cases. Equity lays down that the community as a whole should assist and encourage those who are helping to perpetuate the race by rearing children, care for the orphan, the widow, the sick and the incapacitated, person those who have grown old in useful labour. And Security through Equity will go far to remove the curse of fear and anxiety which is writ on so many faces today.

In the matter of the larger Security which is Peace, the Fascist world-concept is that of independent nations, mutually sympathetic, but as far as possible unfettered by economic or military ties, for fetters sooner or later cause friction. A country which minds its own business, provides for its own defence, and lives, within its own resources, is essentially a peaceful country, giving its citizens the best possible security against the nightmare of war. And this is an axiom which is peculiarly applicable to Britain. The lives of the people are more important than the reputations of international politicians.

RESURGENT NATIONALISM

Fascism is universal, but it is not international. It does not flow outwards across national frontiers from a centre, as Communism flows outwards from Moscow. It springs spontaneously from the soil of each country, and each stream acquires national characteristics, as rivers acquire colour from the land they traverse. The streams may take parallel courses, but they do not merge.

There are several reasons for this. The first is that Fascism is essentially a realist reaction from the illusions of internationalism. For years Socialists have been preaching social and economic reform through international action. For years the League of Nations enthusiasts have been preaching peace through international law. We have had neither reform nor peace. Disillusioned, the people turn back from the shadow to the substance, to grapple anew with the familiar things which lie to hand, to work out their own destiny.

The second reason is the eminently practical one that the nation is quite the most workable unit for purposes of revolution. Its foes are Finance and Communism, both of them inherently international. If it fights them on their own ground, it fights at an enormous disadvantage. If it can detach a national unit from the international web spun by Finance and exploited by Communism, it can build up that unit into a citadel of resistance. If that citadel can achieve self-sufficiency, victory is virtually assured. This helps to explain why Finance is so anxious to get Germany and Italy back into the international debt-system, and why Russia was so enthusiastic about upholding the League of Nations.

The third reason is that the task of reconstruction is infinitely easier when conducted behind national frontiers. When agriculture and industry are free from foreign competition, the just price and the fair wage can be established. When raw materials can be secured without resort to international markets, the nation obtains full control of its own economic life. When the money-system is insulated from international speculation and trafficking, it can be purged of abuses and set to work for the processes of production and consumption. When culture is protected from external influences, the national heritage can be preserved and carried forward.

But the fourth reason is, in many respects, the most important of all. It is that Fascism is fundamentally spiritual rather than intellectual. An international creed must of necessity employ abstractions and formulae, a national creed invokes the age-old appeal of patriotism, going right down to the roots of man in his native soil. Abstract inspiration is reserved mainly for an intellectual minority. While inspiration is born of the real and living, a great hushed crowd, a rich landscape, a noble river or mountain, is for any man to seize. Spiritual renaissance on the grand scale is almost inseparable from national renaissance.

There is something curiously blind and unimaginative about the mentality which writes off racialism and nationalism as "narrow" because they do not fit certain formula. One does not need to prove race purity in order to prove the biological existence of race. The blending of similar stocks, strengthened by generations of common environment, common culture and historical associations, has produced something well worth preserving, something which is unequalled as a basis for common endeavour. It is a rock amid a sea of abstractions, the rock on which Fascism builds its citadel.

We British are a mixed stock, but a stock that has been proved and tempered by centuries of history without invasion and without infiltration of serious dimensions. If we have lost something of our nationhood, it is because we have allowed the international Money-spinners and the facile theorists too much scope. It is the Money-standard which has robbed us in less than a hundred years of that sturdy independence which was once our pride and inoculated us with the curse of parasitism. It is the cult of international theories which vitiates our relations with other countries and fills the headlines with war-scares.

For a nation which cannot feed itself, which cannot maintain its industries, which can move neither wheel nor ship, without the assistance of a score of other nations, is no longer independent. A nation which cannot shape its foreign policy without reference to a cosmopolitan crew at Geneva is no longer sovereign. A nation which cannot change its government or formulate an economic policy without leave of international financiers is halfway to moral bankruptcy. It is exposed to exploitation and blackmail of every kind. It has reached a state of affairs which is not even democracy, it is abdication.

Those who have grown up with this state of affairs and profited by it would have us believe that it is inevitable - a queer and perverted philosophy. Is it inevitable that the plains of Canada and Australia and Argentina should be robbed of their fertility to make our bread? Is it inevitable that the Danes should always send us their butter while they eat margarine? Is it inevitable that the oil fields of Asia and America should drive our trucks and fly our planes? Is it inevitable that the whole world should lay its tribute on our doorstep? Is it inevitable that the world should accept our manufactures, our loans, and our well-meant but often quite impracticable advice? It is an ever-changing world, and there are few things inevitable in it; one of them is that the stupid and decadent must pay the price of their folly and blindness.

Most perverted of all, and highly dangerous in a world which still suffers acutely from war-neurosis, is the doctrine that nationalism is aggressive. This is akin to saying that a man who keeps himself fit is necessarily pugnacious. If sloth, decadence and tolerance of injustice are the only alternatives to aggression, there is indeed little hope left.

RESPONSIBLE IMPERIALISM

Undeniably there is a certain incompatibility between nationalism and imperialism. A nation which is jealous of its own independence and integrity cannot well deny these conditions to others, nor will it be strengthened by the tribute derived from subject races.

Imperialism may, however, be of more than one type. It may be of the colonizing type, which seeks to people sparsely-inhabited lands with its own superabundant population: it may be the military type; which seeks primarily to acquire prestige: it may be of the trade type which seeks to provide more scope for its merchants and financiers; or it may be of the complementary type, which seeks to exchange its administrative skill, and possibly manufactures, for essential materials lacking in its own resources. British Imperialism has been a blend of all four types, with the trade type predominating, for trade has more often preceded the flag than followed it.

Be that as it may. The British Empire is a fact, not to be dismissed with airy generalisations. However it was acquired, it is now our responsibility, and there is no need to apologize for it. There is, however, some need at this juncture to justify it.

There are, of course, three British Empires, the Commonwealth, or loose federation, of white populated sovereign States, the Indian Empire, and the so-called "colonial" Empire of territories in which we rule large native populations. Each requires a different policy.

The Dominions we must cease to regard as economic dependencies just as we have ceased to regard them as political dependencies. Their debts to us, which in some cases are very considerable, call for drastic adjustment as a standing menace to friendly relations. Our financial system, aided as it has been by the loan-hunting propensities of Dominion politicians, has been directly responsible for land wastage on a huge scale, to say nothing of the human wastage of many settlement schemes.

RESPONSIBLE IMPERIALISM

Each Dominion, with the possible exception of little Newfoundland, has for many years past, been aiming at a state of self-sufficiency. It is therefore unreasonable to expect that they will fully maintain their purchases from us of manufactures. At the same time, the long overdue development of our agriculture together with the adjustment of interest payments will lessen our need for their products. They cannot, therefore, reasonably expect us to provide them with an unlimited market, but in so far as we continue to need agricultural imports, we must certainly buy from them in preference to foreign countries.

The old conception of the Dominions as "agricultural" countries providing a market for our goods, food for our people, and an outlet for surplus population, is due for revision. It suggests a state of mutual dependence not strictly in accordance with the facts. It would be far better to regard them, not only as partners in the Commonwealth, but as self-contained communities, with whom, however, we can still exchange goods with advantage. When they are less dependent on their exports to us they will be better able to build up their own populations

Of the Indian Empire it is a little presumptuous for anyone to make suggestions when not personally intimate with the medley of races and creeds which make up its teeming population. But certain things are sufficiently obvious. The first is that Indian "nationalism" is as artificial as Europeanism, and that the projected all-India federation threatens to be a second League as soon as the grip of the British Raj is relaxed. The second is that democracy, already in process of rejection by the Western nations whose child it was, is hopelessly unsuited in any form for Indian conditions: all the evils to which has given sanction in the West, corruption, oligarchy, factionalism, will flourish as the bay tree in the fertile soil of the East. Far more likely to bring peace and prosperity to the Indian masses would be a corporate structure of semi-autonomous communities, held firmly together by strong and impartial British suzerainty. The third is that any weakening of our authority will certainly be followed, not only by internal strife, but by the penetration of other Powers who lack our delicate scruples.

The Colonial Empire, too, consists of native populations which cannot be left to their own resources. Our administration may not be perfect, but it is infinitely superior to any condition likely to follow our withdrawal. And so long as we accept responsibility for administration, there seems to be no valid reason why we should not adapt the resources of their territories to the needs of our Imperial economy. Most of these territories produce tropical commodities which improve our own standard of living, but do not compete with our own producers. They are, on the other hand, a market for manufactured goods, which others are anxious to exploit if we do not. The scope for controlled complementary trade is obvious.

Here again there is a great danger that the imposition of doctrinal formula and exotic systems of government may head these peoples back into the exploitation from which they are now protected. The development of local forms of government under our leadership has much to recommend it; the establishment of self-government for its own sake has little.

Outside the Empire are the ex-German colonies which we hold under mandate from the League. The League being virtually moribund, we have now got to choose between retaining them as acquisitions by conquest and returning them to their former owner.

The former course means a permanent extension of responsibilities which are already sufficiently onerous, and of resources which are already more than sufficient for our needs. It means a legacy of bitterness, comparable to the bitterness of France during the 58 years that she was bereft of Alsace-Lorraine. It means a barrier to that Anglo-German understanding without which there can be no peace in the world. And on the whole it hardly seems worth while. On the other hand, we are still in a position to do the sporting thing, and do it with honour and dignity, not only from motives of expediency, but from a sense of justice. We may not be able to retain that position indefinitely.

The foregoing suggestions will, no doubt, be equally unpalatable to jingoes of the Right as to "anti-imperialists" of the Left. But the

RESPONSIBLE IMPERIALISM

Empire is neither a blessing to be accepted without question nor an evil to be destroyed without question. It is a living, growing organism, and it is our responsibility to see that it lives according to our best traditions and grows in the best direction. Already it is being challenged from within and from without, and an attitude of intransigence will be as fatal as one of abdication. As an imperial race, we cannot just exist; we must either justify our empire or perish with it. And if we can retain at the heart of the Empire but a fraction of the vision and courage which built it and serve it today, justification should be well within our capacities.

REALIST ECONOMICS

Liberal economics broke down because lack of regulation let in the overweening plutocrat. Orthodox Socialist economics fail to inspire for the precisely opposite reason that excess of regulation will let in the overweening bureaucrat. But the basic fallacy common to both is overemphasis on consumption. Both regard man simply as a consuming animal. Thus he reverts to the status of a beast of the field: and ethics and morality can be preserved only in so far as they can be separated from economics; which is an entirely unnatural divorce. The Socialised State certainly pays more heed to Equity, particularly in distribution, but even more than Liberalism does it deny man full expression of his creative personality.

Before economics can become more than a set of conventional formula, it must view man as a whole, as a producer who produces, not only in order to be able to consume, but in order to find an outlet for his creative instincts. It must view work as something more than so much drudgery, so much labour exchanged for the right to live, more even than so much service to the State. It must view the object of economic activity as something more than the consumption of the maximum quantity of wealth, the earning of maximum profits, or the accumulation of the maximum quantity of capital. Above all, it has got to view both Money and Machinery in their proper light as servants of man and not his masters. How far does Fascism give effect to this economic philosophy? Can it deliver us from the gloom and frustration of a wholly materialist economic system?

The first principle of Fascism is leadership, a pre-requisite of economic deliverance. We begin to know vaguely, what we want, but democracy has produced no one who can show us how to get it. Democracy has come to be an affair of parties, and no party can exist without an alliance, direct or indirect, with Finance, wherefore every party politician becomes, sooner or later, an apologist for vested interests, a defender of What Is rather than a champion of What Should Be, still less a prophet of What Will Be. Only a great personal leader, drawing his strength direct from the people, can challenge the power behind the throne.

The second principle of Fascism is team-work, which is surely the key to the economic riddle. The Money monopoly which keeps the community chronically short of purchasing power, the Liberal economic theory which preaches a code of self-interest, the Marxian doctrine which preaches class-warfare, all have contributed to produce a state of affairs in which employer and employee, producer and consumer, engage in an unending dog-fight. Fascism rejects in turn the quantitative theory of money, the self-interest theory of economics, and the Marxian theory of class-warfare. It invokes instead the sense of responsibility inherent in every normal man, and by removing the vested interests which breed sectional strife, mobilises every citizen as a member of the national team.

The third principle of Fascism is national independence, economic as well as political, for no nation can live its own life which depends for its existence upon the vagaries of international trade. So long as it permits foreigners to compete in its own markets, so long as it must compete with foreigners in export-markets, its living standards are in constant jeopardy. So long as it must buy and sell abroad, it is utterly dependent upon International Finance and the foreign exchanges, and must shape its policy accordingly. In short, indulgence in international trade means the sacrifice of national sovereignty.

The transition from international interdependence to national independence, though clearly not a thing to be lightly undertaken, is not nearly as impossible as many people suppose. We are by no means deficient in natural resources: on the contrary we are extremely well endowed. It is the distortion caused by Free Trade which has led to their atrophication. Our land is no more than half worked, even by very moderate standards: many useful coal-seams and mineral deposits have been abandoned or neglected in favour of imported oil and minerals. The possibilities of homegrown fibre, alcohol and timber have hardly been touched. With the immense resources of the Empire to supplement our own, we can achieve a standard higher than the world has yet seen. And though this is not the only or even the first objective of Fascist economy, it is attainable only by the adoption of that economy.

Fascism thus provides a definite break with money-economics and an approach to real economics, the standard of which is not Money but man and his needs. It does not simply invert the capitalist machine as does Socialism, it reconstructs it and gives it new motive power. The precise form which this reconstruction will take will depend upon conditions prevailing at the time of transition; but certain main objectives can be summarised.

Many existing conventions and institutions will undergo profound modification. The consumer-complex, which now operates so unfairly against the most useful section of the community, will give way to a code which seeks to raise living standards by increasing man's status as a producer rather than by making concessions to him as a consumer. The competitive system will continue to operate as a stimulus to enterprise, but will cease to function as a recognised means of forcing down wages and prices.

The price-structure itself will be greatly simplified and modified. The prices of staple commodities will be fixed, and this in turn will stabilise the purchasing power of money: technical improvements in production will be reflected in higher wages and profits; not in lower prices. The price of other commodities, though not necessarily fixed, will tend to come into line, while the corporate structure of industry will check any fluctuation arising from excess or inadequate production.

It follows that trade, as such, will lose much of its present significance. It will cease to be either the objective or the regulator of economic activity, and become more strictly functional. In so far as the trader "produces" useful distributive services, he will find a place in the corporate structure and acquire status as a producer. In so far as he lives by exploiting a variable output and a variable price, he will lose his occupation and will have to be found work in a more useful sphere

The network of interests that is now concerned in international trade will, in particular, be thinned out. This does not mean, of course, that external trade will cease altogether. Empire trade will continue, and expand, and there will be considerable specialised foreign trade. But this trade will become purely supplementary to domestic production and consumption, and will be conducted on a barter basis, goods against goods, with regulated supplies and prices. "Markets" as we now know them will virtually disappear, and with them most of the camp-followers of trade.

Finally, and most significantly, Finance will be brought under strict discipline. Even during the period of transition, there must be rigid control of the movements of capital, both internally and externally. Credit will cease to be available for speculative purposes, and the trade in currencies will be checked. As the policy of autarchy takes shape and the corporate structure develops, the Money system will become more purely functional. Interest on fixed debts will be scaled down until it is eliminated altogether, while dividends on share capital will be subjected to specified maximum.

This policy will have some important repercussions. In the first place, production will no longer be regulated by return upon capital, but mainly by consumptive demand. In the second place, capital investment will no longer be regulated by the rate of interest and the flow of savings, but by the national economic policy laid down by the Corporations under the guidance of the Executive. In the third place, special consideration will have to be given to those who are obliged through circumstances to depend upon invested savings; this consideration might take the form of annuities, pensions, and insurance policies. In the fourth place, debt will no longer be regarded as saleable, income-producing property: in fact the community will be able, for the first time in modern history, to reduce the burden of debt and the servitude which it entails.

Gold will cease to function as the basis of the Money system, though it may be used as a matter of convenience for the balancing of international transactions, its value being assessed in terms of commodities. The fiction of convertible currency will finally disappear, and the volume of currency will depend entirely upon the volume of trade passing. Similarly credit will be issued at nominal interest for productive purposes on the security of the new wealth to be created.

And so at last Britain will throw off the Financial dictatorship which has so long ruled unseen through the solemn farce of democracy, and so long corrupted our nationhood. She will be free at last to use her own unequalled resources and her unequalled technical skill for the enrichment of her own people, asking leave of none as to what course she may or may not pursue. Then at last employer and employee, producer, trader and consumer can make common cause in the fight against poverty, muddle and waste which now disgraces our 20th century civilization.

THE CORPORATE STATE

THERE is a great deal of nonsense talked about the Corporate State, no doubt because the word "corporation" has suffered considerably by modern usage. The Corporate State is neither State nor capitalistic autocracy, nor is it even a. loose federation of syndicated interests. It is essentially an attempt to break away from the mechanistic concepts of Liberalism on the one hand and of Marxian Socialism on the other, and to model national life upon the natural lines of human physiology.

The human body functions as an organic whole. Every organ and every member performs some essential function, and is vitalised by the common blood-stream and nervous system. The brain, certainly, co-ordinates and directs, but it can be said to "dictate" only if it is assumed that its interests are distinct from those of other parts of the body, which is absurd. Conversely, if any organ or member behaves at variance with the rest of the body, then the system is clearly disordered and abnormal. In short, the body corporate is not operated by preconceived theories of liberty and equality, democracy or autocracy, but by the natural processes of organic life.

So in the Corporate State, every member has functions and responsibilities; he shares in the common life, the common task, the common wealth. He may own property sufficient for his needs and appropriate to his position; he may own and employ capital in order to make his contribution to the national welfare. He has rights and privileges, but also duties and responsibilities. The State does not exist for his convenience, but neither is he its servant; he is an integral part of it.

The Corporate structure is built, up on the productive elements of society, by virtue of their qualifications as producers. The individual unit will continue; the factory, the mine, the shop, the farm, will not pass under centralised control; on the contrary, the great combines which now dominate industrial and commercial life will be resolved into very much smaller units. But each industry or group of industries will be co-ordinated and regulated by its own representative Corporation, in which employers and employees will share equal responsibility, and on which the community as a whole will be represented by members of other Corporations or by Government nominees.

Each Corporation will be responsible for wages and working conditions within its own industry, for regulating prices and for adjusting output to demand, and for representing the industry in the councils of the nation. It will by no means stifle competition between its component units, but lay down the rules by which that competition is to be conducted. It thus becomes an extremely practical and effective form of self-government. If industry has got to be "planned," and we are already some distance along that road, this surely seems the fairest way of doing it, and the way most consistent with the independence of British character.

In addition to the industrial Corporations, there will be Corporations representing important non-industrial elements of the community, as for instance housewives, the professions, education, and pensioners. The structure of these will naturally vary, but essentially they will be fasces of persons bound together by a common task and common interests, and holding a common qualification. They will be accepted as expert authorities in their own spheres.

Co-ordinating the whole will be a Council of Corporations, consisting of delegates from each Corporation, under the presidency of a member of the Executive. This Council will naturally become a national economic clearing-house, a symposium of functional experts. It will take over the control now exercised by Finance, and direct the flow of currency and credit. It will take over the technical business now performed, laboriously and circuitously, by Parliament, by Government departments, and by innumerable Committees and Coinmissions. It will be a more effective expression of the will of people than anything which democracy has yet produced, and a more effective instrument of economic government than anything which Finance has yet devised.

With much of the work now thrust upon it entrusted to more

capable hands, it becomes a moot point whether there will any longer be justification for Parliament. Certainly that institution cannot continue as a stage for party maneuvers and licenced loquacity. On the whole it will be desirable to maintain a forum for the discussion of non-technical matters and the ventilation of grievances which do not come within the purview of the Corporations. But it is essential that the geographical system of representation, which means in effect the party system, should be discarded in favour of an occupational franchise. The representation of a rural constituency by a stockbroker, or an industrial constituency by a lawyer, would be utterly inconsistent with Corporate principles. If Parliament is to continue, it must more accurately represent a cross-section of the community than it does now.

Similarly, the allocation of executive posts on purely party lines will be discarded. The system whereby a lawyer can become in turn a Lord of the Treasury, Minister of Agriculture, First Lord of the Admiralty and Chancellor of the Exchequer, is taking gross liberties with the nation's inherent right to effective management of affairs. The Corporate principle, in any case, reduces appreciably the need for Ministerial heads of Government departments, just as the principle of leadership disposes of the Cabinet system. With the democratic system of representation goes the oligarchic system of government.

The King naturally remains as the first citizen of the land and hereditary head of the British Empire. In fact, with the disappearance of the ruling class and the party politicians, to whom an intelligent monarch is anathema, he will obtain much wider opportunities of direct contact with his subjects. The present concept of the Crown as the puppet of an oligarchy is an appalling degradation of the principle of monarchy, none the less disturbing for being camouflaged by an elaborate system of ballyhoo, as the revolt from it of Edward VIII, was camouflaged by a spate of sanctimonious priggery.

In place of a Prime Minister selected by a party caucus bound by party ties, and able to find refuge at need within the party, arises the Leader, responsible directly to King and people. With the focusing of inspiration and responsibility in a central figure, the last justification for a Cabinet disappears, and the Executive becomes the Leader himself with his small group of picked lieutenants.

It is this Executive alone which requires the mandate of a general election, for the Corporate structure, being removed from party strife functions continuously, its constituent bodies electing their representatives in the manner most convenient to themselves. At specified intervals, or on any occasion when a change in policy is required, or whenever a major event occurs unforeseen, the Executive seeks a fresh mandate from the people. Should it fail to obtain a decisive vote, the King exercises his right to send for those in whom he has most confidence, and who in turn must appeal for popular support. Thus the power of recall remains with the people, under the guidance of their hereditary head. The Government serves the King and people, not vice versa.

And so the Corporate State emerges as the full expression of that team-spirit, that abiding sense of loyalty, that craving for national unity, which is inherent in British character and which has been frustrated time and again by the party system and the tangle of vested interests which have grown up with it. It is essentially a totalitarian State, because a team which is divided against itself, is not a corporate body, but only a collection of dissentient groups and individuals. It is the only kind of State which can possibly cope with the tremendous issues which lie ahead with the tremendous opportunities which are ours to grasp, and to throw away the tremendous dangers of despotic international collectivism, and can at the same time provide opportunities for that self-expression which is the birthright of every individual.

EPILOGUE

SPRING ON THE WAY

BRITAIN today is being challenged, challenged not only as a democracy, which is inevitable, but also as a nation, which is ominous. As our orthodox formulae crumble away, as our lack of unity and purpose becomes increasingly apparent, that challenge grows louder and more insistent. It is not so much a challenge by any specific Power or Powers, as a challenge by a world charged with the dynamic and impatient of the static. That world, which once accepted without question our leadership, now queries not only our leadership, but also the permanence of the British Empire. We, who have achieved so much, and who can achieve still more, are held incapable of achievement.

And this challenge is being answered. Not by pompous politicians, not by a hysterical Press, not by turgid discourses on Democracy from platform and pulpit, but by a devoted band of men and women in whom the spirit of Britain still lives. Beneath the crust of old dead things the new life stirs.

British Union was first forged in the furnace of the Great War, when it seemed that we might be purged of the dross with which unashamed commercialism had encrusted the soul of the nation. It was tempered in the years of bitterness and disillusionment, which followed years, which spurned the qualities, which the War had brought forth and seemed dedicated to opportunism and money-making. It required the crisis of 1931 to shape it for action.

The first Fascist movement in Britain started in 1923, the year after Mussolini's March on Rome. It preached Fascist principles, had a strong ex-service element, and attracted much support. But the incipient Bolshevism which it was formed to resist died away, and having few political ambitions of its own, the movement suffered from lack of purpose, as well as from its tendency to become an extreme wing of Conservatism. It was not till 1931 that the portent appeared — Mosley.

By every canon of political orthodoxy Oswald Mosley should by now be a pillar of Conservatism; judging by the calibre of the present Cabinet, he would be its outstanding figure. Scion of one of the oldest land owning families in England, product of Winchester and Sandhurst, he entered the War as a typical young cavalry officer. He emerged from it one of the many who believed that nothing short of a new and better Britain could serve as a memorial to our million dead. He entered Parliament at the "Khaki Election" of 1918, a war veteran of 22, as a Coalition Conservative.

But post-War Conservatism had nothing to offer an idealist, and after a period of independence Mosley joined forces with Labour, not as a disciple of Marx, but as one who believed that Socialism in some form or other most nearly represented the aspirations of the common people. Deserting residential Harrow, he ran Neville Chamberlain to a few votes in his Birmingham stronghold, subsequently won industrial Smethwick at successive elections, and entered the Labour Government of 1929, especially charged, with two others, with the relief of unemployment.

The fate of that government is recent history. Returned by the electors to cure unemployment and work for Socialism, it proceeded with clumsy hands to shore up the very system it was pledged to destroy, while the unemployment figures rose higher and higher. In vain did Mosley urge upon it a policy of reconstruction. It would not accept his plans, it would not produce an alternative, it would not appeal to the country for a decisive mandate. It was sufficient that it had achieved office that Snowden was acceptable to the City of London.

In May, 1930, Mosley resigned his Ministerial post: a man of honour could have done no less. A year later, frustrated at every turn by the Labour caucus, he led out of the party the little group which, with a few progressive Conservatives, formed the nucleus of the New Party. In a matter of months this move was amply justified by the defection of Macdonald, Snowden and Thomas to the ranks of reaction,

With characteristic party logic, the betrayed Labour party turned, not upon the traitors but upon those who had tried to expose the betrayal. Savagely attacked by the hooligan camp followers of Labour, handicapped by its own lack of organisation, the New Party was utterly submerged in the General Election of 1931, which sent a panic-stricken Britain swinging back into the arms of "Sound Finance" and its champions,

Having twice sacrificed his career for his principles, Mosley was not the man to accept defeat. The policy with which he had won his first election, the policy which he vainly urged upon the Labour Party as practical Socialism, was still, to his mind, the right policy for Britain. But bitter experience had shown him that policy alone was not enough. There must be behind it a disciplined organisation which would refuse to be drawn into the party bickering and demoralising compromises of democracy which would refuse to be intimidated by the hooligan element which had wrecked the New Party. Both the policy he upheld and the organisation he needed were clearly of the Fascist type. Hence, the fusion in 1932 of the New Party survivors, with the progressive wing of the British Fascists, to form the British Union.

At first the British bourgeoisie, still badly shaken by the crisis of 1931, was disposed to welcome any opponent of Labour. Funds and publicity were forthcoming, which in turn brought a rush of recruits. But as the revolutionary, character of the movement came to be appreciated, suspicions were aroused. Then came the National Socialist triumph in Germany, which loosed the full tide of outraged Liberalism and vengeful Jewry, and the power of Jewry is by no means to be measured by its numerical strength. From the top came financial pressure which converted good publicity into bad, cut off funds and made it risky for anyone to display open sympathy with the young movement. From the bottom came Yiddish reinforcements for British Union's Red foes, and queer un-English names appeared with monotonous regularity in police records of anti-Fascist violence.

But the challenge acted like a tonic. As the half-hearted and the inevitable adventurer dropped out, the faithful closed their ranks to meet the attack on two fronts, and found new and more lasting support in all kinds of unexpected quarters. Under Jewish pressure, a scared Parliament hastily passed discriminatory legislation which was an open violation of the principle of political freedom it claims to uphold. Uniforms were banned; but uniforms had ceased to matter; the campaign for public recognition had been won.

And so British Union, in the first six years of its life has won two important battles, the first against the obvious temptation to become a picturesque appendage of reaction, the second against a situation which facilitated the manufacture of propaganda against it. It has yet to win a third battle, against the political apathy which has been sedulously fostered by years of minority rule; but with the threat of war and the imminence of the next slump, it will have powerful aids to the removal of that apathy.

Most important of all, it has learnt from adversity where the fight for Britain must be fought and won. Just as Fascism builds upwards from national traditions so British Union is building upwards from the roots of society. In the thousands of poor homes where men and women face the grim realities of life, in the little shops which lie beneath the shadow of the chain-stores, on the little farms where hope long-deferred, embitters honest toil, in the great army of sweated labour which provides the luxuries of plutocracy, British Union is entering the lives of people.

The struggle approaches its climax. As the artificial prosperity of the loan-boom reaches bursting point, as the burden of debt and taxation slows down the wheels of production, as party politics reveal their sheer incompetence to keep pace with the quickening tempo of world-change, there will be a rallying of the vested interests round the democratic standard. Die-hard Liberal, cosmopolitan financier, doctrinaire Socialist and vengeful Communist, every adventurer who exploits the licence which Democracy provides, will man its last citadels. There will be a reckless expenditure of abuse and propaganda, and not a little licenced violence, as this highly variegated Pseudo-Popular Front turns at bay in defence of its precious formulae, its carefully preserved rackets, and, above all, its self-made jobs.

But there never was a spring without some wild weather, without a bitter north-easter, as winter slackens its grip. And no more than these rearguards of winter can stop the bursting of the bud and the up-rush of the young leaf-blades can the rearguards of reaction stop the renewal of national life. British Union marches on.

Spring comes again!

Lightning Source UK Ltd.
Milton Keynes UK
UKOW052251080313

207382UK00006B/197/P